SUCKING UP

Sucking Up

A BRIEF CONSIDERATION OF SYCOPHANCY

Deborah Parker and Mark Parker

University of Virginia Press

CHARLOTTESVILLE AND LONDON

University of Virginia Press
© 2017 by Deborah Parker and Mark Parker
All rights reserved
Printed in the United States of America on
acid-free paper

First published 2017

ISBN 978-0-8139-4089-2 (cloth)
ISBN 978-0-8139-4090-8 (e-book)

9 8 7 6 5 4 3 2 1

Library of Congress Cataloging-in-
Publication Data is available for this title.

Cover photo: iStock/mayakova

CONTENTS

SUCKING UP

Introduction

Unbelievable, unbearable, incomprehensible. Sucking up takes a variety of forms, from petty compliment to oily flattery to outright treachery. Our responses are just as varied—from annoyance to disgust to rage. Sycophancy is everywhere, combining with other vices: hypocrisy, lying, manipulation, and fraud. Is there any limit to its reach?

Perhaps not. Consider the 2006 episode in which Vice President Dick Cheney, vacationing at a ranch in Texas, emptied his shotgun into the face, neck, and upper torso of a fellow hunter and friend. (One uses the term "hunter" loosely, given the fact that the two were shooting quail released from pens.) Although spokesmen for Cheney were quick to blame the victim, Harry Whittington, it's clear that the fault rested with the shooter, who aimed downward, at dusk, toward an uncertain target. Whittington's wounds were much more serious than original reports by those close to the shooter let on: he suffered a collapsed lung, considerable inflammation from the shot (most of which he still carries in his body), and a mild heart attack. His speech has been affected by a piece of shot in his larynx. Yet Mr. Whittington emerged after a week in the hospital to offer this fantastic statement: "My family and I are deeply sorry for all that Vice President Cheney and his family have had to go through this week." This display of obsequiousness boasts an imaginative scope few acts of sycophancy can match. As a matter of fact, Cheney seemed to "go through" very little after the incident. His hostess reported that the vice president was laughing about the shooting over cocktails later that evening. Whatever trouble Cheney's family endured can only have been minimal, except perhaps for the embarrassment caused by the media's likening of the patriarch's marksmanship to that of Elmer Fudd. However, Whittington appeared to think that Cheney was owed an apology from not only himself but also his family. In a final burst of servility, the victim concluded: "We hope that he will continue to come to Texas and seek the relaxation that he deserves."

What might Whittington have expected from such abasement? Perhaps the better question is, What retribution did he seek to avoid? One might pause over such a statement, suspecting a note of mockery in offering familial as well as personal regrets, but nothing Whittington has said subsequently suggests any hint of tongue in cheek. And the former vice president, as in so many cases, has valiantly chosen not to speak about the pain the memory of shooting his friend in the face might have caused him.

In any case, the Whittington kowtow—in part because of its absurdist humor—helped to move Cheney and the Bush administration past the questions raised by the shooting. Cheney's unavailability to investigators the night of the accident, his level of intoxication (whether through alcohol, prescription medicines for his heart condition, or a combination of both), the political calculation that dominated the management of the incident— all these considerations gave way to amusement. In retrospect, Whittington's aim was true, even as Cheney's was not. This episode, at least at the time, seemed an extreme case in the annals of Washingtonian sycophancy, an uncanny literalization of the "take one for the team" ethos so familiar in government.

But our current moment outruns this efficient quid pro quo model of sycophancy, rivaling the bootlicking of courts, monarchies, or even the most absolute despotisms in intensity and frequency. Consider the case of Kellyanne Conway, the successful manager of Donald Trump's campaign and a longtime Republican activist. After her boss complained on Twitter of unfairness after several department stores dropped his daughter's line of clothing, Conway appeared on network television to urge Americans to "go buy Ivanka's stuff." Let's set aside the fact that such a pitch violates a rule for federal officials. It's the pettiness of the flack that boggles the imagination. Buying Ivanka Trump's clothing line would contribute absolutely nothing to Trump's campaign pledge to "make America great again," yet the newly appointed "counselor to the president" found time, in the early days of a historically chaotic transition of government, to peddle a failing line of clothing. Conway later spoke eloquently of her relationship to the president in another ecstasy of bootlicking: "His message is my message. His goals are my goals."

Or consider Press Secretary Sean Spicer's memorable defense of Trump's insistence on the size of the crowds at his inauguration. On the first day of his new job, one that requires trust between the spokesperson and the press, Spicer antagonized reporters with repeated lies. Spicer was obtuse and aggressive, but his actions were clearly sycophantic, an early display of his berserker loyalty to his new boss. And his truculence in itself was a testimony to Trump's signature manner.

Or consider Chris Christie's luncheon with the president at the White House, at which the president, in a characteristic display of schoolyard dominance, ordered for the governor (though not for anyone else present). "Was it emasculating?," Christie was asked in an interview. Hardly. "It is the president," chirped Christie, again proving himself a ready and adept sycophant. Note the lack of argument; the appeal is delivered as if it were self-evident. Of course one submits. And the job-seeking governor went still further: "And the meatloaf was good." As yet, no job has emerged for the able and willing Christie, but, if it does, he appears to have the resiliency and good humor requisite for the rigors of Trump's sycophantic regime. The meatloaf, one assumes, will always be good, whatever else the flatterer must eat.

The sycophancy cultivated by our new president has not gone unremarked. But, as it becomes the master trope of the Trump era, a consideration of the practice is in order. We clearly will see an extravaganza of fawning, flattering, and flunkyism over the next few years, and we should take the widest possible view of this practice in order to despise it properly.

"Fittest Imp of Fraud"

We can never know the origins of many of our most familiar behaviors. Indeed, they often have no distinct beginning, only a gradual emergence from a hazy past. Yet we imagine them anyway, as primal scenes that shape our experience of the world. And what these stories lack in plausibility or simple truth, they make up for with insight into our preoccupations, values, and beliefs.

So we might ponder one of the central moments of *Paradise Lost,* John Milton's story of the beginnings of human history, to wonder at what this seventeenth-century Protestant revolutionary adds to the biblical account of the fall of man. Surprisingly, amid the usual elements of disobedience, sin, and damnation, Milton inserts another all-too-human failing—sucking up. As Satan pursues his revenge on God by corrupting humankind, he meditates on his own fall as well as the further depths of degradation that his plot requires. Satan takes two forms—serpent and sycophant—in deceiving Eve. The physical form he assumes disgusts him:

> O foul descent! That I who erst contended
> With gods to sit the highest, am now constrained
> Into a beast, and mixed with bestial slime,
> This essence to incarnate and imbrute,
> That to the highth of deity aspired.[1]

Satan loathes his fallen form, from airy spirit seated at God's side to slithering reptile. But the serpent, "fittest imp of fraud" (bk. 9, line 89), is the perfect means for the sycophantic attack Satan plans on Eve. In the yet-unfallen world, the serpent still possesses a strange beauty. His approach, pleasing and alluring in every motion, suggests the sidelong, hedging actions of the expert toady:

He bolder now, uncalled before her stood;
But as in gaze admiring: oft he bowed
His turret crest, and sleek enameled neck,
Fawning, and licked the ground whereon she trod.
(bk. 9, line 523–26)

Fittingly, it is the devil himself who introduces sycophancy into the world, and humankind's first experience of evil and deception takes the form of flattery. Milton shows a wry sense of humor here, in fashioning the first sycophant into an emblem of bootlicking. Satan literalizes a familiar figure of speech for sycophancy, licking the ground, reenacting what was, by Milton's time, already a cliché.

The prominence of sycophancy in Milton's account is astonishing. Later in the encounter with Eve, the archfiend argues forcefully that eating the fruit would make Eve and Adam gods as well, and that God unjustly withholds the fruit of the tree from his creatures. This might be the most reliable weapon in the sycophantic arsenal, that the target "owes it to himself" to act selfishly or to transgress. Milton might have simply presented Satan as a masterly speaker who deceives the hapless Eve. But he insistently frames Satan's malicious fraud with sycophancy. Even more suggestive is Milton's emphasis on the body in his presentation. The words we often use for sycophancy—ass-kisser, brownnoser, lickspittle—revel in this connection between flattery and filth. The Prince of Darkness cannot convey his disgust for his actions without recourse to the "slime" of a cloying physicality. He rings the changes on "beast/bestial/imbrute" with concentrated force, expressing the depth of his revulsion with flashy wordplay.

Milton's account of the first flatterer is compact but rich. We see how vulnerable innocence is to ingratiation. We see how effective such manipulation can be. We also see how it feels—or perhaps *should* feel—to be a sycophant. And we glimpse something of how catastrophic its effects are—here nothing less than the fall of man.

Word Sounds and Histories

The Sounds of Sycophancy

Satan's disgust notwithstanding, some words just seem fitted for what they name. The pleasure of saying "sycophant" is immense. The word rolls delightfully off the tongue. One's lips purse and expand. The *s* sound, the result of the friction of the breath in a narrow opening, provides a hissing contempt. The *k* sound that follows—the effect of a sudden release of air—is clipped and accusatory. The mouth, in making the *f* sound that follows, curls with disdain. One almost spews the word. The *f* and *s* sounds are related (as voiceless fricatives), so the *f* seems to return to the opening *s*. The *n*, the last of the word's root sounds, makes its own satisfying return to the opening *s*—both are technically alveolars. The interplay among these root sounds gives the word unusual density. There is much to savor in the physical act of calling someone a "sycophant."

Such pleasures, oddly, extend to the many synonyms developed for sycophancy in English. Suck-up, lickspittle, ass-kisser, bootlicker, and brownnoser all open with an emphatic explosive syllable, and they feature a gratifying play of sounds between the opening syllables and those that follow. There is a melodious quality to such words, from the repeated sibilants of "ass-kisser" to the more intricate repetitions of "lickspittle." One may relish pronouncing someone a "sycophant," even as the concept passes through many translations and recoinages. To charge someone with sycophancy has a ceremonial aspect—we smear as we pronounce.

Charivari

In addition to providing the sonic pleasures of its internal rhyme and alliterations, a coinage like "lickspittle" delights the eye—or at least the mind's eye. To charge a cringing sycophant with lapping up spit summons a gratifying image, at once grotesque, excessive, and humiliating. The variety and rough humor of these ingenious coinages amount to a public shaming. Like the charivari of old Europe—raucous communal processions used to shame husbands or wives who did not meet certain standards of behavior—such language not only says something; it also *does* something.

Consider the rich spectacle of "ass-kisser" or its close relative "brownnoser." One focuses on the absurd act itself, the other on an equally absurd consequence of such an act—a telltale residue that announces sycophancy. Think of the damning literalism of "yes-man," which reduces sycophancy to mindless monosyllabic compliance. Yet another playful coinage, "toadeater," adds strangeness to nastiness. Performances in themselves, these insults are acts of both aggression and invention, weapons and entertainment.

Origins of Sycophancy

Nowhere does the progression of time seem more erratic than in the history of words. Derivations, which seem to promise clarity by offering a roadmap to the origin of a word, almost never deliver an authoritative meaning. Yet the life and times of a word can be suggestive. We can locate the first appearance of συκοφάντης (*sykophantes*) in sixth-century Greece, where the legal system allowed informants to bring action against lawbreakers and to profit from their convictions. The earliest meaning of the word would be "meddlesome informer," something like a cross between an ambulance chaser and a whistleblower.

The fourth-century Greek dramatist Aristophanes pursues this meaning in his comedy *Plutus*, or *Wealth*. Chremylus, the poor and just protagonist of the piece, meets Sycophant, whom the god of wealth has stripped of his possessions. Chremylus questions Sycophant, who insists on his honesty and civic-mindedness. His actions are not those of the "vile intriguer." He serves the state by "watching that the established law is observed." In fact, according to Sycophant, "all public affairs fall within my province."[1] Aristophanes emphasizes the rapacity and bustle of Sycophant, who, however pestilential, has the cover of law for his aggression. Flattery and fawning do not form a part of Aristophanes's characterization. His sycophant is more intrusive and insolent than servile. The Greek language itself supports this distinction, providing another word for simple flattery, κόλαξ (kolax/kolakeia). Latin maintains this separation as well; sycophanta, which retains the Greek sense, is distinct from adulator or adsecula, terms for flatterer. The first uses of the word in English, in the mid-sixteenth century, begin to fuse these two meanings.

While the usage of sycophant is easily established, the derivation is speculative. The most common explanation suggests that the Greek word blends φαίνω (to show) and σῦκον (fig), and that the combination reflects a historical circumstance. The importation of figs was forbidden, and the state rewarded those who rooted out smuggling. This dovetails with the "meddlesome informer" usage. But another account sees the word as metaphoric, suggesting that a sycophant knows how to find the fruit. Yet another possible derivation relates the word to the practice of "giving the fig"—an obscene gesture—which emphasizes the hostility of the sycophant. Each derivation—informant, opportunist, and aggressor—gets at something essential to a full understanding of sycophancy. A word with a complex derivation suits a complex human activity.

Cautionary Tales

Excremental Visions

Often sycophantic anecdotes turn more on disgust than amusement, and they work less by variation than spectacular excess. Saint-Simon (1760–1825), whose *Memoirs* chronicles life in the late eighteenth-century French court, records an instance of truly world-class sycophancy for posterity. His gossipy account of the Duke de Vendôme's insolence, laziness, sexual abandon, and filthiness includes a detailed description of the duke's morning routine. Upon rising, the duke took up his "chaise percée" (a portable toilet), upon which he held court for hours, sending and receiving dispatches, seeing visitors, and eating breakfast. The duke delighted in treating visitors, especially aristocrats whom he considered to be of lesser rank, with disdain.

During the French occupation of northern Italy, the Duke of Parma sought to lighten the burdens placed on the populace by the forced maintenance of Vendôme's army. Vendôme met the duke's ambassador, a bishop, in his usual style, sitting in state on his chaise percée. During the interview, he rose, turned his back to the bishop, and wiped himself. Disgusted, the bishop refused to see him again. However, diplomacy is the art of finding a way, no matter how foul that way might be. The bishop found the perfect substitute for these negotiations: the superserviceable Giulio Alberoni, who had risen from poverty though a series of clerical appointments. Alberoni, treated to the same display by Vendôme, had a ready reply: "O culo d'angelo" (roughly translated, "Oh, ass of an angel!"), and he "ran to kiss" the duke's behind. Sycophancy seems to have served Alberoni well. He later became consular agent to Philip V of Spain, rose to cardinal in the Church, took part in the conclave that elected Innocent XIII as pope, and was himself proposed in the next papal election. He received a respectable ten votes.

It's hard to say whether this anecdote is entirely true. And true or not, a literal reading might miss the wit of Alberoni's quip or perhaps the shrewd opportunism with which such courtiers employed sycophancy. But it certainly fits our expectations about the excremental excesses of sycophancy. Nor does this episode stand for the limits of ingratiation. An anecdote from the Han dynasty (206 BCE–220 CE) concerning the fabulous rise of Deng Tong in the court of Emperor Wen, again involving a favorite's zealous sycophancy beyond the call of duty, easily surpasses the Alberoni story. The emperor suffered from a tumor, which Deng Tong undertook to keep clean by sucking the pus from it. Such abasement is remarkable in itself, but perhaps equally astonishing is the use to which Deng Tong reportedly put this filthy bit of service. Emperor Wen asked Deng Tong who loved the emperor best. The sycophant suggested that his heir would have the deepest affection. So the emperor quickly employed his heir as royal pus-remover. The heir, showing understandable distaste for this task, lost favor. Deng Tong, of course, reaped the benefit of this brilliant stratagem in competitive sycophancy.

One other Chinese anecdote shows the ingenuity with which obsequious flatterers can transform the basest of bodily functions into an ecstatic experience. This one is from a collection of jokes from the fifteenth or sixteenth century: a scholar dies and meets the king of the underworld. The king, sitting on his throne, farts loudly. The scholar writes a short poem on the spot. It goes something like this:

> Raising high your exquisite buttocks,
> you released precious air in generous amount;
> vaguely the sound of thread and bamboo as if the smell of musk
>   and orchid;
> standing to the leeward, your servant smelled,
> the most pervasive fragrance.[1]

So gratified is the king that he grants the versifier another ten years to live. But when the scholar appears before him again, the king, recollecting his honeyed words, rebukes him as a flatterer. This judgment relegates the scholar to the first of the eighteen levels of Diyu, the Chinese Realm of the Dead. The first level is reserved for those who used language fraudulently—slanderers, liars, the glib-tongued, and flatterers. Their punishment, not unlike those in Dante's *Inferno*, draws on the notion of contrapasso, or counterpenalty—the punishment fits the crime. In Diyu, ghosts use pliers to pull the sinner's tongue from his mouth.

Modern times are no less rich in stories about the servility of lickspittles. A Soviet anecdote goes like this: Brezhnev (general secretary of the Communist Party in Russia, 1964–82) is lying at the beach surrounded by Communist Party flatterers, each one trying to outdo the other in praising his genius. Finally he gets tired, sends them away, and lies down on his face to rest. A dog comes up and begins licking his bottom. Without turning around he says, "Now really, comrades, that's a bit much."

The present, of course, has its own stories. A colleague from a California university sent us this story concerning a powerful provost who had surgery for hemorrhoids. On his first day back a faculty member sent him an inflatable ring pillow to sit on in the office. Perhaps the motive was genuine solicitude, but the gift came so close to literalizing the traditional trope for sycophancy that only a particularly tone-deaf aspirant for favor would have risked it—or perhaps an exceptionally witty one.

Such fables testify to how low flatterers may stoop in their relentless pursuit of favor. They seem, by their exaggeration, to strip bare the nasty reality of sycophancy, even as they offer, in retelling, some humorous consolation to those who have witnessed it. However, they prevent us from thinking more constructively about brownnosing. The response to such an extravaganza is always another such story. This kind of contest short-circuits any serious consideration of the practice. Extreme examples—such as Deng Tong's pus sucking—might be amusing to recount, but they obscure, by their incredibility, the familiar forms that sycophancy takes in everyday life. Intimate, subtle, and ubiquitous, sycophancy—especially the kind we see every day—deserves

TV CALIGAS INFLARE MEAS, EGO CVDERE NVMMOS

The Man with the Moneybag and His Flatterers, Jan Theodor de Bry, after Pieter Bruegel the Elder, 1661–63. (National Gallery of Art, Washington, D.C.)

closer attention. What are the motivations of sycophants? What are the wider effects of their actions? And what is the larger meaning of this simpering practice?

Damned Flatterers

Technically, Dante's Hell does not present sycophancy as a separate category of sin. Malebolge, the eighth circle of Hell, has ten divisions, which include panderers and seducers, flatterers, thieves, sowers of schism, falsifiers, and hypocrites, among other sinners. The modern conception of sycophancy combines many of Dante's categories of fraud. But a rose by any other name smells as sweet—or in this case, stinks as foully. Modern readers of the *Inferno* recognize sycophantic behavior in the two flatterers named in this circle—Alessio Interminei, a courtier from Lucca, and Thaïs, a courtesan in Terence's comic play *Eunuchus*.

Dante's punishment for flattery—immersion in shit—exploits the long-standing association of flattery with excrement. Full of crap while alive, in death they are plunged into it. The poem also indulges in the rough humor often accorded flatterers and sycophants. Dante mocks Interminei's filthy condition by quipping, "I have seen you before / with your hair dry,"[2] and the sinner's response—to pat his shit-covered head—heightens the jest. The description of Thaïs displays carnivalesque excess as well. Virgil, the Roman poet who guides Dante through Hell, directs his charge's attention to:

> . . . the face
> of that besmirched, bedraggled harridan
> who scratches at herself with shit-filled nails,
> and now she crouches, now she stands upright.
> That is Thaïs, the harlot who returned
> her lover's question, "Are you very grateful
> to me?" by saying, "Yes, enormously." (*Inf.* 18.129–35)

Her flattery lies in her boundless exaggeration. Thanks would have been sufficient, but the flatterer always inflates her response, under the impression that an excess of gratitude may yet elicit more gifts in the future.

Dante, as he consigns sinners to grisly punishments on his descent through Hell, is often graphic in his descriptions. Here his language is downright crude. Excrement abounds in this episode, but Dante casts even harsher light on Thaïs as she scratches herself with "shit-filled nails." Even the word Dante uses for excrement—"merda"—is a dramatic departure from the usual language of epic poetry. Flattery inspires a coarser treatment and coarser language.

The power and clarity of Dante's images, like the extravagance of the Alberoni and Deng Tong episodes, can easily distract us from *Inferno*'s deeper themes. But amid this disgusting display, we might note that what Dante terms flattery (and what we might call sycophancy) lands the sinners deeper in Hell than sins such as tyranny, heresy, or even murder. How, we might ask, is Thaïs worse than Attila the Hun or Alexander the Great, tyrants who "plunged their hands in blood and plundering" (*Inf.* 12.105), but whose crimes are punished above in the seventh circle of Hell?

Dante, whose sense of community was powerful, reminds us of other ways of thinking of human experience. Sins that are variants of fraud—lying, hypocrisy, flattery—have effects that go beyond the immediate situation. Fraud creates a culture in which all interaction is suspect, in which simple frank exchange cannot be taken for granted. Fraud debases the community in which we move, creating uncertainty, doubt, and distrust. Dante's valuation of flattery initially shocks us, but it also forces us to consider the damage fraudulence does. Murder, so long as it stops short of a war of all against all, has limits. We know it for what it is at once. Fraud, by casting a shadow on all interaction, is endless.

The Will to Power and Sycophancy: Henry Kissinger

The damage done by pervasive fraud—even if only of the sycophantic variety—is clear from Dante's *Inferno*. But Dante's flatterers are types—emblems that stand for abstractions in the larger scheme of the poem. At times Dante gives us intricate psychological portraits of the sinners that the pilgrim meets in Hell, but there is no depth to the flatterers. Alessio Interminei and Thaïs—a courtier and a courtesan—are small cogs in Dante's greater wheel of Christian doctrine. We assume their flattery because of their place in the *Inferno,* and we respond to them accordingly. They don't tell us much about how flattery works.

But what, then, about sycophants and flatterers in the real world? Might true stories tell us something that fictional accounts do not? Let's trace the effects of wholesale sycophancy by following the career of an exemplary sycophant. In *This Town* (2014), Mark Leibovich called Washington "Suck-Up City." No surprise here: like cats to cream, politicians turn to flattery. Likewise lobbyists, strategists, and agents are heat-seeking missiles for funding. Insider Washington, with its power hostesses and would-be power brokers, works the same way. Although it would be difficult in this cesspool of bootlickers, hypocrites, and other assorted pond scum to identify Suck-Up City's flatterer-in-chief, Henry Kissinger would surely be a top contender.

Largely known as a prominent advisor on foreign affairs from 1969 to 1977 and as national security advisor and secretary of state under Presidents Richard Nixon and Gerald Ford, Kissinger is currently chairman of his consulting firm, Kissinger Associates. Born Heinz Alfred Kissinger in 1923 in Fürth, Germany, Kissinger became a naturalized American citizen in 1943. After serving a stint in the army working for military intelligence, he got his bachelor's degree from City University of New York and did graduate work at Harvard. He joined the faculty of Harvard's Department of Government after finishing his PhD in 1954.

Kissinger honed the skills by which he would become influential (and infamous) while a graduate student at Harvard— mastering foreign policy, playing both sides of rivalries, currying favor with power brokers by flattering them slavishly. As director of the Harvard International Seminar, Kissinger invited world leaders, bankers, and writers to spend the summer at Harvard. He beseeched speakers as diverse as Eleanor Roosevelt, the poet John Crowe Ransom, and the labor leader Walter Reuther to participate in his seminar—Would they be kind enough to lecture to his students?[3] These were the beginnings of a global network that Kissinger would expand over the next fifty years to include titans of industry, socialites, and Hollywood power brokers. His smug brilliance and adeptness at sucking up to powerful people prompted fellow students to take his middle initial, *A*, and call him Henry Ass-Kissinger behind his back.[4]

Fast-forward to Kissinger's unholy alliance with Richard Nixon. Before being asked to be Nixon's national security advisor, Kissinger discussed with Gloria Steinem how he would respond if asked to serve. Having supported Nelson Rockefeller, Kissinger had an aversion to Nixon. Steinem invited him soon after Nixon's election to write a piece for *New York* magazine that would address "the collaboration problem," a subject Kissinger understood well, having analyzed the Austrian statesman Klemens von Metternich's collaboration with Napoleon in his dissertation. (Metternich arranged the marriage of an Austrian archduchess to the general after a détente between the two countries.) In his thesis, Kissinger asked rhetorically: "To co-operate without losing one's soul, to assist without sacrificing one's identity[,] what harder test of moral toughness exists?"[5] What harder test, indeed?

By the 1960s Kissinger had become a master at ingratiating himself with those in a position to further his career. He was particularly adept at flattering rivals—to "cooperate," as he put it. His ability to charm, to make someone feel that he or she was the only person he could trust, was legendary. At Harvard he had deftly plied William Yandell Elliott and Carl Friedrich, rivals at Harvard's Department of Government. He routinely cooed to journalists: "I know you're the only one covering me who will understand this."[6] Before Hubert Humphrey lost the 1968 presidential campaign to Nixon, the cooperative Kissinger wrote Humphrey a fawning letter offering his assistance if he was elected. No less flagrant were his deceits. As John Lehman (Kissinger's congressional liaison and secretary of the navy under Reagan) once quipped: "You can't for long convince [both] Katherine Graham and Jesse Helms that you're secretly their soul brother."[7] While it's hard to imagine Kissinger as anyone's soul brother, the incongruity of Lehman's figure of speech nicely emphasizes the gap between Graham, the liberal publisher of the Washington Post, and Helms, the reactionary and segregationist senator from North Carolina.

Kissinger applied his skills as courtier to perfection with Nixon. After a meeting with his boss and Soviet ambassador Anatoly Dobrynin, Kissinger gushed to Nixon himself: "It was extraordinary! No president has ever laid it on the line to them like that." Before an April 1971 speech on Vietnam, Kissinger sent the president a handwritten note: "No matter what the result, free people everywhere will be forever in your debt. Your serenity during crises, your steadfastness under pressure, have been all that have prevented the triumph of mass hysteria. It has been an inspiration to serve. As always, H."[8] A paean to Nixon's serenity. Nice touch.

Various biographers had unmasked Kissinger as a consummate adulator. But the release of the Nixon Tapes confirmed that there is no Rubicon to be crossed by some sycophants, only the question of how deep to plunge themselves into the currents. After the first batch of tapes was released in October 1999, newspaper articles decried what had long been known but not exposed so extensively—Nixon was a thoroughgoing bigot and anti-Semite. Here's one such exchange from the summer of 1971, in which Nixon's inner circle, gathered in the Oval Office, indulges in a bit of Jew bashing:

"But Bob [H. R. Haldeman, chief of staff], generally speaking, you can't trust the bastards. They turn on you. Am I wrong or right?"

[Haldeman agrees]: "Their whole orientation is against you. In this administration, anyway. And they are smart. They have the ability to do what they want to do—which is to hurt us."[9]

Similarly, Charles Colson, a political operative widely known as Nixon's "hatchet man," readily provided his boss with a list of the ethnicities of workers in the Bureau of Labor Statistics after its director, Julius Shiskin, had reported an upswing in unemployment. As Colson rattled off the names, Nixon thundered, "They are all Jews?" "Every one of them," Colson readily agrees. "Well, with a couple of exceptions. . . . You just have to go down the goddamn list and you know they are out to kill us."

In Haldeman and Colson we have fairly run-of-the-mill yesmen, appeasers chiming in as needed when Nixon ranted about the "traits" of various races and ethnicities—the Irish "get mean" when they drink, Italians "don't have their heads screwed on tight," Jews "are very aggressive and abrasive," and blacks had to be "inbred" to advance in society. Such rancid generalizations are well known to anyone who has studied the prejudices of this famously paranoid and secretive president.

It remained to Kissinger, however, to pander most reprehensibly to the Bigot in Chief. On May 1, 1973, Golda Meir, then prime minister of Israel, had a meeting with Nixon in the Oval Office during which she asked him if Americans would be willing to ask the Russians to allow more Soviet Jews to emigrate so that they might escape further persecution. After Meir left, Nixon and Kissinger had a debriefing. In the midst of a discussion of the president's negotiating style and Meir's request, Kissinger made it easy for Nixon to refuse Meir, declaring: "The emigration of Jews from the Soviet Union is not an objective of American foreign policy. And if they put Jews into gas chambers in the Soviet Union, it is not an American concern. Maybe a humanitarian concern."[10] While the first of Kissinger's points might constitute an argument about policy, the vehemence of the hypothetical—particularly when produced by a Jewish refugee from Nazi Germany—goes far beyond the requirements of even realpolitik. "In New York, the epicenter of Jewish life in the United States, some jaws are still not back in place after dropping to the floor," reported the *New York Times*.[11] And unlike Haldeman and Colson, who were prompted by Nixon's anti-Semitic remarks and readily chimed in, Kissinger needed no cue.

Although some Jewish newspapers defended Kissinger's remarks by claiming "he had to go the extra mile to prove to the president that there was no question of where his loyalties lay," and drew attention to his more positive achievements (debatable as those might be for many), the majority registered outrage. Kissinger has since argued that his taped comments "must be viewed in the context of the time."[12] Sycophancy doesn't get uglier than this. *Maybe* putting Jews in gas chambers is a humanitarian concern? Even Nixon never went so far as to cast a blind eye to a repetition of the Holocaust.

Nixon had a tape-recording system installed in the White House in early 1971, but only a few close members of his staff knew about it. Kissinger only learned about the tapes two months before their existence was revealed by Alexander Butterfield, a White House aide, during the Watergate hearings. As Walter Isaacson, whose biography of Kissinger was published eight years before the release of the Nixon Tapes, keenly observed, "Nixon's White House tapes, when they are finally released, will be particularly damaging to Kissinger because they will show him fawning over even Nixon's most hair-raising notions." In 1982 Kissinger ran into John Ehrlichman (counsel and assistant to Nixon for domestic affairs) in Los Angeles and admitted, "Sooner or later those tapes are going to be released, and you and I are going to look like perfect fools."[13]

Just fools? One might return to Kissinger's remark on Metternich's collaborations: "To co-operate without losing one's soul, to assist without sacrificing one's identity[,] what harder test of moral toughness exists?" Kissinger meant it, in its original context, as high praise for his subject—praise that other scholars have withheld from Metternich. But to turn that question on Kissinger himself is another matter entirely. It becomes the measure of his loss of moral identity.

Ultimately, despite the thousands of pages Kissinger wrote about his diplomatic career—sometimes to clarify, at other times to exculpate or evade—his sycophancies still confound observers. We can apply rough judgment easily (and Christopher Hitchens does just that, by simply listing Kissinger's maneuvers in his book *The Crimes of Henry Kissinger*), but we cannot account for Kissinger's stunning and repeated capitulations to Nixon or his collaboration with various strongmen and dictators in their pursuit of antidemocratic and tyrannical policies. His motives, like those of Dante's flatterers, remain beyond us.

The Science of Sycophancy

A Pioneering Study

The limits of biographical or historical accounts of sycophancy are clear. Can we find some illumination from science? Academic researchers have taken great interest in ingratiation. This attention began in the middle of the last century within departments of psychology and sociology, but over the next fifty years it shifted almost entirely to business schools. This change underscores the centrality of sucking up and other forms of what researchers call "Impression Management" (IM) to the modern workplace, or at least the workplace that MBA programs imagine for their students and faculty—that is, offices at some distance from the realm of material production and manual labor.

A field of study is often defined by an early work that sets out a general theory of the phenomenon, poses questions for future research, and offers a method for pursuing these inquiries. Edward E. Jones's 1964 *Ingratiation: A Social Psychological Analysis* is just such a work.[1] A paradigm for research on sycophancy, Jones's study identifies three basic kinds of ingratiation—other-enhancement (that is, the classic suck-up), opinion conformity (the yes-man), and self-presentation (the self-promoter). Through a series of experiments, he sets out the main concerns of future research—the relative efficacy of these different kinds of ingratiatory behavior, the effects of power on success in ingratiation, the ability of both target and sycophant to recognize the ingratiatory behavior in which they are involved, the effects of ingratiation on an observer, and the risks of various strategies of ingratiation. Even today, fifty years after the publication of Jones's study, researchers still cite his work, frame experiments based upon his assumptions, and seek to replicate his claims.

Jones begins by reminding us that ingratiation is always "interpersonal"—it involves at least two and often three people. This permits different perspectives on the behavior. An act of ingratiation "can mean one thing to the actor, another to the target of the action, and still another thing to a neutral observer" (2). Another variable complicates these interactions further: the sycophant himself can be unaware of his sycophancy. Jones further notes, with some amusement, that it is difficult to ascertain the "normative base line from which ingratiation departs" (3), that is, what differentiates an act of ingratiation from simple friendliness. He offers two criteria, "manipulative intent and deceitful execution" (3), but he admits that these are only helpful if one can know them to be the case—which is precisely the difficulty. To determine bad faith, whether from the target's perspective, in which the same behavior can be either ingratiatory or not, or the actor's perspective, in which he might well deceive himself as to his culpability, is always tricky and often impossible.

Let's consider the implications of these assumptions. Since sycophancy depends upon unknowable intentions and ambiguous actions, empirical research is bound to be imprecise and inconclusive. The study of ingratiation must determine both whether a behavior is ingratiatory and how conscious both target and actor are of the act as ingratiatory. We have to know what the act is, and we have to know what everyone involved thinks it is. Moreover, as sycophancy becomes more effective, it also becomes harder to pin down. Both act and intent are inscrutable because both the act and the intent are in play.

Jones's conclusions do not stray far from traditional notions about ingratiation. He first explores the sycophant himself. Jones notes that people are easily induced to suck up, that they readily deceive themselves about the nature of their activity, and that a "hunger for approval" underlies both the action and the self-deception. And of course the target believes the flattery to be sincere as well. Sycophancy ultimately requires a willingness to deceive and be deceived on the part of both parties, as if each is "anxious to believe the [ingratiatory] better than he really is" (79).

Second, Jones considers the circumstances under which ingratiation takes place. The decision to suck up depends upon the value of the perceived rewards, the probability of success, and the current level of acceptance of sycophancy. Jones then examines the role of power in sycophancy, more specifically how a disparity in status between flatterer and target shapes the behavior and its interpretation. Finally, Jones turns to the target, whose response to flattery ranges from naïve acceptance and reciprocation to toleration, annoyance, and disgust.

Jones's analysis is objective, but his attitude is not impartial. He often acknowledges and sometimes quotes from treatments of sycophancy in literary texts, such as Lord Chesterfield's *Letters* and Plutarch's *Lives*. These mentions are not simply embellishments or asides; Jones praises their authors' acuity, and he accepts their moralizing. The cynicism of Jones's account of ingratiation—often leavened with a benevolent humor—draws on a rich literary tradition.

Along the way Jones, with conscious irony, makes several recommendations for aspiring bootlickers. Yes-men should take care to disagree with the boss occasionally, but only on irrelevant things. Similarly, flatterers should mix criticism with praise—but making sure in each case to reserve their negative remarks for things of no importance. Sophisticated yes-men can enhance the perceived value of their conformity by making a show of initial resistance to the target's opinions. And sometimes flattery is most effective when delivered not as simple praise, such as enthusiasm for a trait or ability, but in relative terms, such as, "you are much better than your boss/rival/coworker" at some task. In fact, flattery is often best delivered indirectly, by a third person, if that can be managed.

Jones also notes, somewhat mischievously, the risks that sycophants take. Flattery from a position of equality or dominance almost always works, but the same remarks or gesture from a subordinate might simply mark him as a lickspittle. For the underling, opinion conformity is always safer, but one runs the risk of proving oneself pathetically deficient in leadership capacity. Despite the vulgar physicality of the many euphemisms for sycophancy, great discernment and some real daring are required before one can properly place one's tongue on the boot.

Jones's emphasis on performance pays off throughout his analysis. In distinguishing ingratiation from convivial social exchange, he writes: "The ingratiatory presents himself as a party to one kind of exchange—with one set of terms and conditions—while he is in fact primarily involved in another kind" (12). This is a suggestive formulation. It makes ingratiation remarkably like irony, a literary figure in which an expression says one thing and means another. The transgression of ingratiation is not simply one of bad faith, like an outright lie. Ingratiation, like irony, bends language, and in doing so, it might exceed our ability to recognize it. Irony, when obvious, becomes sarcasm; ingratiation, when clumsy, becomes simple bootlicking. Sarcasm can sting, and bootlicking can disgust, but both lack the corrosive power of successful irony or ingratiation. A successful act of ingratiation darts between two realities, and in doing so confounds the target, sometimes the observer, and even the flatterer himself.

Jones brings a broad humanism to his research. His conclusions tend to echo traditional ideas about sycophancy—in fact, his work is best viewed as an inquiry into method rather than a presentation of particular findings. None of his claims have the éclat of a TED Talk—that razzle-dazzle combination of counterintuitive novelty and measured takeaway. Jones begins with curiosity—perhaps even disinterested curiosity—and, under his steady gaze, sycophancy, so familiar to us in anecdote and in story, becomes more and more strange. The more he seeks to quantify or measure sycophancy, the more elusive it becomes.

Jones's modesty is refreshing. He readily concedes the limitations of his study in the conclusion to *Ingratiation*: "Our use of the laboratory experiment cannot at present be justified as a part of a strategy of cumulative theoretical confirmation" (197)—that is, the reach of his theory far exceeds the grasp of any experimental method. Even as the phenomenon has a "lively history in literary discourse" (203), it eludes scrutiny in the lab. When Jones returned to his work on sycophancy in a later book, *Interpersonal Perception* (1990), his sense of the difficulties in investigating sycophancy had deepened. Once "evanescent" (201), now the phenomenon becomes downright obscure. He reconsiders his earlier definition of sycophancy only to marvel at the paradoxes of this behavior.

> [Ingratiation] exploit[s] the logic of social exchange while subverting it. The goal of being liked merely because one has made an effort to be liked can best be attained only if it is concealed.[2]

Sucking up works best when its essential quid pro quo goes without saying. The parties involved carry out an exchange that they tacitly agree not to articulate. Sycophancy involves a kind of magic that transforms a transaction into something else—preferably something that is never mentioned.

This new emphasis on the transformative power of sycophancy lends Jones's remarks a darker tone. Sycophantic behavior that he dismissed as ludicrous in his earlier book, he now finds more troubling. What was once a consciously considered plan carried out by the ingratiatory now becomes enigmatic. When Jones returns to his account of the calculations that every sycophant must make as he sizes up his prey, he notes the self-delusions to which the prospective toady is subject. The lickspittle will still weigh the "incentive value" of the act—that is, whether the outcome would be worth it. He will still gauge the "subjective probability of success"—whether it will work. And he will still take into account the morality of the behavior, the "perceived legitimacy" of the action, or, in other words, the question of how fraudulent and inauthentic the behavior will make the prospective bootlicker feel. Jones still relishes the flatterer's perplexity. But upon reflection he adds that the last variable might regulate the first two considerations. While a sense of shame might nip the toady's obsequiousness in the bud, it might also lead the sycophant to modify his expectations and actions in ways that appear more authentic, both to himself and to the target. In other words, the sycophant can harness any residual sense of morality, however fleeting, to refine his technique. Morality is not so much a curb as an invaluable tool for the sycophant. A truly shameless bootlicker would be less effective than one who uses his sense of shame to hone his skills.

As the old saying goes, "The secret to success is sincerity. If you can fake that, you've got it made." For the sycophant, that ability to deceive is paramount, both with respect to the target as well as one's self. Sycophancy, according to Jones, shapes the sycophant. What was once simply concealment of one's motives from others quite easily becomes concealment of one's aims from oneself.

These mystifying conspiracies of disavowal lead Jones to push the logic of his position further: "Ingratiation is illicit because it bypasses the open channels of social exchange, but . . . the strategic character of the ingratiator's behavior does not typically involve conscious awareness or deliberate planning. It is strategic, it is illicit but it remains cognitively inaccessible" (*Interpersonal Perception*, 178). With these last words, Jones neatly predicts the failures of later research on ingratiation. The subject can never be precise about his motivation or intentions. You can't ask the subject; you must find an experiment that captures such actions in ways that also distinguish them from other behavior. Using surveys and interviews is problematic, since they require interpretation of the information. The ambiguities of life persist in the controlled spaces of the lab: "We know these things as lay observers, perhaps, but they are difficult to grasp conceptually and not easy to realize as experimental variables" (199). Later researchers, however, have not been so scrupulous about the inherent limitations of laboratory experiment.

From Ingratiation to Image Management

As mentioned previously, the study of sycophancy has migrated since Jones's time from psychology departments to business schools. Such a move is predictable. Given the ambiguities of detecting flattery and the obvious dangers of "opinion conformity," one would expect that bosses would be interested in ferreting out sycophants. Presumably the study of business methods should include such research. But the assumptions made by many of these studies and the attitudes they take toward their subject are disconcerting. Recent research often stresses the utility and even necessity of sycophancy for the ambitious, effectively studying sucking up not so much to understand it as to put it to good use. While researchers are not shy about using blunt terms like sycophancy, flattery, or "the slime effect," they subsume these activities within the less denigrating category of "impression management" (IM), and they often conclude their presentations of research with what looks like advice. Whereas curiosity led Jones to the study of sycophancy, IM research displays more pragmatic motivation. With this emphasis on utility and immediate application, IM work seems to lose interest in the humanistic questions raised by Jones's work and ultimately even the phenomenon itself. For Jones, the study of ingratiation "brings into relief some of the central mysteries of social interaction" (*Ingratiation*, 16), and his work leaves us with ambiguities, puzzles, and methodological complexities. IM work wants a "takeaway" that leads to satisfactory results.

For instance, a recent article in the *Journal of Management Studies* begins by reminding its readers that ingratiation "is the most pervasive influence strategy in the workplace."[3] Such an assumption is well within the area of research set out earlier by Jones. But where Jones proceeds out of a disinterested desire to understand this perplexing behavior, this study simply accepts sycophancy as the norm and seeks actionable results. As the authors say, "it is important to untangle the complexities in the ingratiation processes and outline for whom exhibiting ingratiation is the most beneficial as well as develop practical implications by identifying leverage points to successfully execute ingratiation strategy" (992). Let's unpack this suspiciously euphemistic language. In simple English, "leverage points" are presumably vulnerabilities and weaknesses that the sycophant exploits. Taken together, the deceptions of flattery become a successful "ingratiation strategy." It is one thing to note that sycophancy is pervasive; it is quite another to embrace it. Throughout the article, the sycophant is assumed to be fully conscious of his behavior, which is purely instrumental and happily free from any moral implications. The problem of ingratiation is simply one of implementation: How can one know whether the target has sufficient acuity to catch the flatterer in the act of flattering? The article recommends that potential sycophants carefully evaluate their bosses before launching an ingratiation campaign, and target only those superiors who have "low" political skill. In other words, one needs to carefully match the coarseness of the flattery to the stupidity of the employer. Moreover, employees with sycophantic aspirations should brush up on their own capacities. "Employees who execute ingratiation," the authors advise, "should also attempt to substantially develop their political skill through training and socialization" (1013). The article does not specify how one would find such "training," although, given that the authors assume that sycophancy is "pervasive" in the workplace, perhaps one would only need to keep a close eye on one's fellow workers.

Other investigations recommend more complicated tactics in the "leveraging" of sycophancy. A 2010 article in the *Journal of Marketing Research* argues that even "insincere flattery" (which, the authors note, "*abound[s]* in the market context") can be effective.[4] Targets—here, customers—have two reactions to flattery, one conscious, which recognizes the flattery and ignores it, and one unconscious, which "continues to exist" alongside the negative attitude. Pressed for time, or burdened by simultaneous tasks, a customer might revert to the unconscious, initial reaction: "Although flattery may have a negative impact in the short run, the implicit reaction may still be more influential in some ways than the corrected judgment—both with regard to delayed effects and in terms of withstanding an attack—thus offering further room for optimism to marketing agents interested in using flattery as a persuasion device (while simultaneously being a cause for concern from the consumer's viewpoint)" (131). The authors conclude with some advice for flattery-averse consumers who might wish to protect themselves. They might try "pairing the flatterer with a negative image" (132), which, one supposes, might be picturing the flatterer as licking one's spittle, boots, or ass. But the article makes a strong case for simply carpet-bombing customers with compliments. If confused, tired, or distracted, they might recall even the grossest blandishments favorably. Presumably, as half-aware consumers luxuriate in the pleasures of flatteries remembered, they will prove more ready to spend.

In addition to providing advice on tricking customers, IM research turns repeatedly to the perils of the interview situation, in which ingratiation proves both effective and routine. A 2010 study in the *Journal of Applied Social Psychology* asserts that of the three standard "mediating processes" in the interview—that is, criteria for hiring—two can be addressed by employing various kinds of ingratiation. The writers assure applicants that "it is better to use any type of IM tactics in the interview than to use no tactic at all."[5] Another study concludes that interviewers note and evaluate candidates' IM performances, which they consider accurate indications of ability for the many jobs that require interpersonal skills. "Honest ingratiation," as they term it, like faking sincerity, is perfectly acceptable. "Honest" here presumably means that those involved are in on the game—they simply nod and wink at the skill others show in the arts of flattery. In fact, "what actually matters for interviewers when evaluating applicant[s] are their own perceptions of applicants' IM tactics and not the applicants' actual use of IM."[6] Interviewers with less political skill often mischaracterize ingratiating behaviors as "honest"—that is, not manipulative—and they often mistake the candidate's intent entirely. In fact, more sophisticated interviewers might consider an applicant's level of skill in sycophancy to be a good indication of future job success. Apparently, there is a robust market for skilled sycophantic workers who can exploit "leverage points" with clients or superiors. This brisk pragmatism scours sycophancy clean of any moral considerations. Everyone, it seems, is in on the game—at least everyone who matters—and the display of sycophantic behaviors simply advertises an applicant's skills in deception and manipulation.

Often IM recommendations concern timing. An article in the *Journal of Managerial Psychology* reminds its readers that, while ingratiation works well both initially and over time, it is especially potent "in the earlier stages of a relationship."[7] "New employees," the authors conclude, "would be wise, then, to recognize this small window of opportunity and to 'act' accordingly"

(281). Clearly, one needs to develop one's IM skills as early as possible. Another recent article assumes that ingratiation is one of the skills that employees in the modern, "fluid" workplace need "to proactively adapt and navigate the social context of the work environment."[8] Unfortunately, the authors' survey of interns and bosses reveals significant failures in flattery by young interns. To address this deplorable gap in bootlicking expertise, they recommend that business schools pay more attention to honing their students' skills. After all, "being able to ingratiate effectively seems to be an important key to being well liked by your supervisor, which, in turn, elicits higher performance ratings" (582). Only the inept, those with low political skill, are designated as sycophants; the fast-moving world of modern business requires supple, alert workers who can "leverage the ingratiation influence resource and execute and deliver it effectively" (570).

While some IM researchers deliver their findings with the distance or disdain one might expect given so dismal an account of the modern workplace, recent research has largely assumed that the question is not whether to kiss ass but how to do so effectively. The moral questions so prominently raised by Jones's account of the inherent duplicity of flattery—that the ingratiator invokes one set of rules while playing by another—seem irrelevant. Such tactics are so common that the investigators seem uninterested in or possibly incapable of even imagining a workplace free of such behavior. The research does not so much concern the detection of ingratiation but rather the ways in which flatterers might avoid discovery. The larger questions Jones poses—those concerning interpersonal relations generally—have given way to simple considerations of best practices in flattery, self-promotion, and obsequiousness.

If the aims seem suspect in recent IM research, the methods these researchers employ are even more questionable. Studies rely heavily on questionnaires. Typically, researchers query targets (bosses and interviewers) and those most likely to "leverage the ingratiation influence resource"—the employees and prospective employees who answer to them. The possibility of capturing so complex a human behavior as ingratiation by such means is never discussed. If, as Jones asserts, the same behavior in different circumstances can be either sycophantic or benign, and if ingratiators can be either aware or unaware of their ingratiation, it is difficult to see how asking respondents whether or not a behavior is ingratiatory would be a reliable way of gathering information about it. The situation is little better in the lab, where most studies rely on college students who play roles or evaluate scripted presentations.

Ingratiation is neither automatic (although an inveterate flatterer's swiftness of response might approach that of a reflex action) nor a simple act undertaken at will. Sucking up is a highly social behavior that is intimately connected to language. It is not always recognized, and it resists measurement. Like a joke, one either gets it or one is the butt of it. We should never forget the complexities of such a behavior. Whether we prefer to consider sycophancy in broadly human terms, as an important part of interpersonal behavior, or in terms of success in the workplace, it might be best to learn about it through literature, the subtlest language we know.

The simulations of life in history or biography, or the even more controlled imitations of life in the lab, have severe limitations. Fortunately, some of the greatest works of literature plumb the depths of sycophancy with surprising precision. These stories constitute thought experiments calculated to explore the mysteries of sucking up. Literature concentrates, clarifies, and, even if it arrives at no specific conclusion or resolution, insists that we respect the complexities of human experience.

Literature and Sycophancy

The Flatterer's Playbook

Plutarch's essay "How to Tell a Flatterer from a Friend" provides us with one of the most lucid accounts of sycophancy. A Greek moralist who lived from 46 or 47 AD to about 120 AD, Plutarch influenced many writers, among them Montaigne and Shakespeare, who both drew heavily on his *Lives* and *Moralia*—the former writer praising, the latter happy to plunder. A Platonist who shied from his master's abstractions, Plutarch is less concerned with ideal forms and mathematics than moral questions encountered in everyday life.

Plutarch is famous for the clarity of his exposition. He carefully sets out the nature of both the sycophant and the target, and he is unsparing to each. Sycophancy begins in the target's self-love, which impairs his judgment. Because "everybody is himself his own foremost and greatest flatterer,"[1] that is, complacent and trusting to his virtues, the sycophant need only second and celebrate this flatterer within. The sycophant, on the other hand, has "no nature, no abiding-place of character to dwell in." He takes the shape of his target's desires, ultimately leading "a life not of his own choosing but another's, moulding and adapting himself to suit another" (281).

For Plutarch, friendship—which we all desire and delight in—enables sycophancy. Flattery often "coincides with friendship" (275), making the two in many respects indistinguishable. Sycophants exploit this ambiguity deftly. Friendship often begins in a similarity of taste; a flatterer carefully mimics his target's disposition and preferences. He shares, enthusiastically, his victim's pleasures, interests, or ambitions. If genuine friends are useful and attentive, the flatterer vies to outdo them in helpfulness. An effective sycophant employs all the behaviors of a friend—except concern for the character of one's friend.

The most insidious sycophants, in fact, manage to counterfeit even this, the most valuable aspect of friendship. If true friends find ways to encourage virtue in their friends, and even at times to criticize them, the sycophant will ape this behavior by reproaching only insignificant failings. The imitation is almost complete, and so convincing in its detail that it can barely be distinguished from the original.

Like Dante, Plutarch points out the wider effects of sycophancy. The damage to the immediate victim is obvious, but the consequences for the community, while profound, are obscure. The flatterer not only alienates the target from his friends, but he also creates conditions under which genuine friendship is impossible. A sycophant "thinks he ought to do anything to be agreeable, while the friend, by doing always what he ought to do, is oftentimes agreeable and oftentimes disagreeable, not from any desire to be disagreeable, and yet not attempting to avoid even this if it be better" (295). Ultimately, hollow compliment, cajolery, and smarm drive out frank talk: "In fact it is those who follow a higher ideal and show distress and annoyance at the errors of their friends, who fall under suspicion" (289). In this poisoned atmosphere, it becomes impossible to tell friend from flatterer.

Plutarch recommends that we test friends in order to distinguish them from flatterers. He lists several methods, both active and passive. One might vary one's opinions; a flatterer will shift as one turns. A flatterer will support ignoble, mean-spirited, or vicious actions. A flatterer will undermine one's other friends. But ultimately, the only sure defense from sycophancy is that "we eradicate from ourselves self-love and conceit. For these, by flattering us beforehand, render us less resistant to flatters from without, since we are quite ready to receive them" (349).

While "how-to" elements dominate this analysis, one may also discern several sobering implications. As Plutarch urges in another essay, "In all cases it is useful also to seek after the cause of each thing that is said" (147). Correctly identifying causation is especially difficult in the case of the adroit sycophant. Because the flatterer apes the actions of a friend, his behaviors are often indistinguishable from them. Only knowledge that a person *is* a sycophant allows for the proper interpretation of the behavior.

Thus Plutarch, like so many philosophers in the Greek tradition, leaves us enlightened but frustrated. His techniques for distinguishing flatterers from friends are demanding and possibly inconclusive. More importantly, while the surveillance he advises might catch a flatterer, it also might undermine a legitimate friendship.

Sycophancy Staged

It might be true, as his contemporary and rival dramatist Ben Jonson noted, that Shakespeare had "small Latin and less Greek," but few writers have made so much out of the classics. Plutarch was a favorite source for Shakespeare, who pillaged *The Parallel Lives* for his Roman plays. Nowhere does T. S. Eliot's sly quip that "immature poets imitate; mature poets steal" apply more fully than in Shakespeare's adaptations of Plutarch's work. Shakespeare filched plots, ideas, and phrases, mostly from Thomas North's English translation of Plutarch's *Lives*. In fact, Shakespeare's thefts are more like acts of ravenous feeding; he ingests his classical sources, and they reappear, transfigured, in the muscle, sinew, and bone of his plays.

Consider, for instance, Hamlet's testing of Polonius, a prominent courtier in both Hamlet's father's court and the new court ruled by his uncle Claudius. The entire structure of *Hamlet* echoes the argument of Plutarch's "How to Tell a Flatterer from a Friend," as Hamlet tries the faith of various characters. When the serviceable Polonius comes to fetch him in act 3, scene 1, Hamlet applies one of Plutarch's recommended tests for flatterers—to vary one's opinions and note the flatterer's response:

> *Ham.* Do you see yonder cloud that's almost in shape of a camel?
> *Pol.* By th'mass and 'tis, like a camel indeed.
> *Ham.* Methinks it is like a weasel.
> *Pol.* It is back'd like a weasel.

Ham. Or like a whale.
Pol. Very like a whale.[2]

Hamlet concludes, rightly, that Polonius conspires against him, cajoling him in order to manage his anger at his uncle's theft of the throne. Nor is Polonius the most egregious toady in the court. Shakespeare devotes a long stretch of a later scene to a similar encounter with Osric, a "waterfly" so sycophantic that, as Hamlet jests, "[He] did comply, sir, with his dug before a' suck'd it"—that is, he bowed politely to his mother's nipple before nursing. The play's preoccupation with sycophants and opportunists (or, as Shakespeare more colorfully puts it, time-servers and trimmers) is balanced by Hamlet's deep attachment to Horatio, whom he praises as poor, plainspoken, and philosophic in his indifference to "Fortune's buffets and rewards."

Hamlet's flatterers, given the Plutarch treatment, are exposed. But Shakespeare takes pains to stress how this behavior corrupts court life. Only violent change—the deaths of the entire royal family and the assumption of power by Fortinbras, an outsider— can purge the castle of this debasement.

There is little optimism in an ending that relies on a force that simply sweeps away the old regime. But *Hamlet* is not Shakespeare's darkest depiction of sycophancy. He returns to this theme in *Othello* with even greater pessimism. Here Shakespeare emphasizes the power of flattery to go undetected. Hamlet can't avoid sycophancy, but he can, as Plutarch advises, expose it. In the figure of Iago, Shakespeare goes far beyond Plutarch's grim account.

Even if Othello faithfully applied Plutarch's tests, he would be unlikely to discover the perfidy of the heinous Iago. On the contrary, Iago's ability to mimic sincerity during such trials would assure Othello of his friendship. So convincing is Iago's performance that Shakespeare must take care to tell his audience that he is evil. His villain confesses his treachery in the opening scene in no uncertain terms. "I am not what I am," he confides to Roderigo, yet in spite of stating this bald truth he continues to successfully flimflam his lesser victim. Without such a clear declaration, the audience would be likely to see Iago as offering Othello the kind of friendship that Plutarch celebrates as "the most pleasant thing in the world" (275).

Iago turns Plutarch's analysis into a playbook. He begins to cast indirect aspersions on Othello's wife, Desdemona, by staging a series of apparently frank responses to information that he draws from Othello about her relations with his lieutenant, Michael Cassio. Broken speech—often a repetition of Othello's words—hesitancy, reluctance to pursue the topic, and feigned surprise all serve to undermine Othello's confidence in his wife. The Moor demands more from Iago:

> thou echo'st me,
> As if there were some monster in thy thought
> Too hideous to be shown. Thou dost mean something.
> (3.2.106–8)

Iago's mastery of the repertoire of flattery turns "airy nothings" into facts. Words are not the main source of information here: Iago says very little. But his halting speech and oblique questions suggest a great deal to Othello.

But Shakespeare does not simply present Othello as a hapless victim. His brilliance is to show point by point that Othello's knowledge of the kind of protective measures recommended by Plutarch creates certain vulnerabilities as well. Here Othello evaluates Iago's performance, in particular his reticence and broken speech:

> these stops of thine fright me the more;
> For such things in a false disloyal knave
> Are tricks of custom; but in a man that's just
> They're close dilations, working from the heart,
> That passion cannot rule. (3.2.120–24)

Note the paradox here. Othello could not be more correct in his general understanding of sycophancy. He grasps the essential indeterminacy that any successful act of flattery turns upon.

The same observed behavior can mean one thing or another—in fact, one thing and its opposite. Othello is knowledgeable—even philosophical—about the workings of sycophancy, but this does not protect him from Iago. Plutarch recommends certain tests for flattery; Shakespeare shows how sycophants can turn these into evidence of friendship.

Access to the sycophant's aims and motivations is difficult in Plutarch's essay, requiring painstaking investigation and analysis; but in Shakespeare's play it is impossible. He dramatizes this obstruction in ways that are remarkably thorough. For instance, Plutarch advises close attention to the flatterer's behavior over time, in which inconsistencies, if recorded, can show the intention behind their deeds. By contrast, Shakespeare's play reminds us how complicated this process really is—in real time, perhaps impossible. While Iago's inconsistencies are apparent to the audience, they are not to Othello, primarily because he, unlike the viewer, is not privy to all of Iago's dealings or his true thoughts. The play reminds us that any given character's range of experience is limited, and the comprehensive lucidity that Plutarch prizes is not always possible. Plutarch imagines a world of social exchange that allows time and opportunity for close investigation; Shakespeare shows us a world of constraints, narrow views, and missed clues.

As Hamlet famously puts it, the play, in fact, is "the thing." The dynamics of drama allow for insight that moral essays or everyday experience obscure. Plutarch's analysis of flattery, however acute, does not account for the intensity of feeling involved in discriminating sycophancy from friendship. It's one thing to warn, as Plutarch does, that the flatterer can ape or mimic friendship. But in *Othello* one sees this and also feels it, in the pity and fear with which we watch the degeneration and ultimate destruction of a noble character. Consider Iago's brilliantly improvised response to Othello's threat of violence:

> O monstrous world! Take note, take note, O world,
> To be direct and honest is not safe.
> I thank you for this profit, and from hence
> I'll love no friend, sith love breeds such offence. (3.3.377–80)

Iago invokes the privilege of friends to offer frank advice, and he considers Othello's aggressive reaction to his concern one of life's sad lessons. The truth-teller, according to Iago, is often despised. The intensity of this appeal, combined with Iago's knowledge of the subtle workings of sycophancy, gives Othello pause, and this hesitation gives Iago just enough room to continue his manipulation. But for the audience, Iago's plea is imbued with deeply philosophic assumptions about the value and responsibilities of friendship.

Nor does Plutarch account for the narrow confines of a given relationship. Viewers (or readers) of *Othello* draw on a wide range of Iago's activity, which makes the viciousness of his flattery obvious. But Othello's experience is far more limited. Social life is always partial; the comprehensive view that art affords is a kind of fiction in itself. For the individual, crucial decisions about flattery turn upon a leap of faith. Othello's anguished outburst to Iago—"I think my wife be honest, and think she is not; / I think that thou art just, and think thou art not" (3.3.384–85)—is often the lived reality of sycophancy. The situation admits of nothing between the extremes of true or false, is or is not. And, as in many plays by Shakespeare, the truth finally emerges not through the efforts of good people to see clearly, but through the overreach of evildoers, whose schemes become far too convoluted to sustain. It is not so much that the protagonists restore order as that the illusions created by sycophancy collapse. The truth emerges amid the ruin of the formerly noble Othello and the death of his innocent wife. Flattery is the primary force in the play's action. Sadly, the good characters recognize it only when it is too late to act upon this knowledge.

The Sycophantic World Order

If *Othello* tells us how corrosive sycophancy is, Shakespeare, in *King Lear*, schools us in how pervasive it has become. A play like *Lear* has many themes, but it turns on an analysis of sycophancy. Nothing could make this clearer than the opening scene. Lear, eighty and eager to pass on the burdens of kingship, arranges a ceremonial division of his realm among his three daughters. Before relinquishing the crown, however, he requires that each of his three daughters perform a very public act of sycophancy by answering his question: "Which of you shall we say doth love us most?"

This deeply misguided demand sets the tragedy in motion. The evil older daughters, Goneril and Regan, vie with each other in groveling declarations of their love for Lear. For Goneril, her father is "dearer than eyesight," and her affection "no less than life." Regan, rising to this display of competitive sycophancy, goes even further: "I profess / Myself as enemy to all other joys"—a sentiment that must come as some surprise to her husband, who stands nearby. Cordelia, the youngest, disgusted by their exaggerations, chooses silence, and Lear promptly disinherits and banishes her. Lear's faithful advisor Kent, who objects vociferously to the proceedings, is exiled as well. Sycophancy carries the day, and, as a consequence, the play ends with the entire royal family dead and the surviving good characters utterly dispirited.

As such, the play seems simply to embody Dante's harsh judgment of flattery. But Shakespeare goes beyond straightforward moral condemnation of sycophancy to show how pervasive sycophancy changes the way we see the world. *King Lear* is not simply a lament for some past society of authentic service and loyalty in which patron and client have well-defined duties toward each other. The play provides a horrifying look at a world in which sycophancy is not the exception but the default position.

Shakespeare addresses the corruption of vision in one of the less well-known exchanges of the play. Kent, Lear's faithful but banished counselor, has returned to the king's service in disguise. When Lear falls out with Goneril, he sends Kent with letters to his next eldest, Regan, complaining of his ill treatment and announcing he will stay with her. Goneril sends Oswald—the most zealously willing courtier in this play of flatterers and parasites—to persuade Regan not to receive their father. The two messengers arrive at once. Kent confronts, challenges, and beats Oswald. The brawl attracts Regan and her husband, Cornwall, who interrogates both messengers.

The ensuing exchange turns upon the question of loyal service and sycophancy. Kent defends his assault on Oswald as an outraged response to his fawning and fraudulence. Predictably, his complaint falls upon deaf ears. Kent, exasperated, then insults Cornwall and his retinue:

> I have seen better faces in my time
> Than stands on any shoulder that I see
> Before me at this instant. (2.2.93–95)

This remark could not be more insolent—"I don't like your face." Furious, Cornwall orders that Kent be put in the stocks. But Cornwall's anger does not keep him from making a surprisingly wise comment about the nature of sycophantic behavior. Kent's rejoinder, to his mind, is less frank speech than a subtle appeal to the appearance of frankness.

> These kind of knaves I know, which in their plainness
> Harbor more craft and more corrupter ends
> Than twenty silly-ducking observants
> That stretch their duties nicely. (2.2.101–4)

While the language here is obscure, it's clear that Cornwall prefers his sycophancy obvious and uncomplicated—"twenty silly-ducking observants," that is, a gaggle of cringing, hat-doffing geese— and he finds deeper treachery in plain speech. For Cornwall, Kent's frankness is a "garb," a ruse he adopts that is itself a kind of sycophancy. In a world rife with sycophants, honesty cannot be understood except as another move within a corrupt system. "Plainness" is, in Cornwall's cynical view, treacherous, because it obscures motivation. Obvious flattery, because it reveals itself as such, is less menacing. Here is a world that functions according to another system: whatever is said becomes false. Once sycophancy becomes pervasive, we lose the ability to discern truth.

So corrupt a vision of how the world operates deserves consideration. Cornwall expects sycophancy, flattery, self-interest, and lies. Nothing, including honest speech, is as it seems. Dante addresses the prevalence of fraud in his *Inferno*, but he suggests that, at least in time, it will be recognized as such. Plutarch, while mindful of the snares and intractability of flattery, trusts that vigilance can contain it. Shakespeare provides a much bleaker view of sycophancy: that it obscures and ultimately makes frank behavior impossible. Sycophancy is not simply corrosive. It is like the universal acid of old science fiction—it eats through every container, every precaution.

Fun with Flatterers

Caricature seems made for the depiction of flatterers and flattery. Its basic elements—reduction to a single attribute or gesture, which is then exaggerated and repeated—not only convey the demeaning nature of the act but also distance the reader or viewer from it. Slime in itself is disgusting; slime at a remove can be amusing.

There is, in fact, a kind of joy that we take in observing a sycophant—so long as we know that the person is a sycophant. Telling friend from flatterer is a difficult and often fraught process, but watching the moves of a known toady, and especially anticipating them, makes for great comedy.

Jane Austen's *Pride and Prejudice* is full of amusing caricatures, but none is more powerful than her depiction of the Reverend Mr. Collins, an impossibly smug suck-up who arrives at the home of the protagonist, Elizabeth Bennet, early in the novel. Mr. Collins, besides his good fortune in being heir to the Bennet estate, has secured a cushy benefice. Collins's adulation of his benefactor, who is herself a caricature of aristocratic pride and license, amuses Mr. Bennet, who reads his letter of introduction to the family. Collins writes: "I have been so fortunate as to be distinguished by the patronage of the Right Honourable Lady Catherine de Bourgh, widow of Sir Lewis de Bourgh, whose bounty and beneficence has preferred me to the valuable rectory of this parish, where it shall be my earnest endeavor to demean myself with grateful respect towards her Ladyship, and be ever ready to perform those rites and ceremonies which are instituted by the Church of England."[3] While "demean" here has a primary meaning of "comport," the unfortunate resonance of "cringe" or "abase" clearly strikes the discerning ears of Elizabeth and her father. Mr. Bennet concludes his reading of the letter with an ironic quip, which signals to the quick-witted Elizabeth that Collins is fair game for clever sallies. "Can he be a sensible man?" she asks her father, who replies that he looks forward to observing more of Collins's "mixture of servility and self-importance" (64). The entire family chimes in upon hearing the letter, allowing Austen to reveal their characters as well. Collins's absurd sycophancy is a touchstone, allowing the reader to judge Elizabeth's sisters and mother.

At dinner, Mr. Bennet continues to explore his heir's sycophancy. In describing his patron's sickly daughter, Collins credits himself for his flatteries, which, in an excess of abasement, he professes himself "bound to pay" (68). Mr. Bennet at once pursues this line of inquiry, asking Collins whether his flatteries are spontaneous or studied. Collins could not be more forthcoming about his technique: "They arise chiefly from what is passing at the time, and though I sometimes amuse myself with suggesting and arranging such little elegant compliments as may be adapted to ordinary occasions, I always wish to give them as unstudied an air as possible" (68). Mr. Bennet's amusement, discreetly shared by Elizabeth through occasional glances, could not be more complete. We see how closely attuned father and daughter are here, and how different they are from the rest of the family. And we are, if we take the time as readers to follow the irony and innuendo of Mr. Bennet, equally amused and no doubt gratified by being included in this select circle.

Austen's account of flattery is straightforward. Collins's sycophancy is obvious to the more intelligent characters in the book. No one is confused or perplexed by his behavior. The characters are oblivious to Collins's flatteries, accepting of them, or amused. We seem to be in a world where the dangers of sycophancy are limited, or at least unsurprising. But Austen changes the mood subtly and then more harshly. Mr. Bennet's initial delight in putting Collins's inanity on display wanes, and he finds that his guest will pursue him, with his tiresome prattle, even into his study, the inner sanctum in which he finds refuge. Later Elizabeth finds that beneath

Collins's servility and awkward compliments lies a boundless confidence in his own value. He asks her to marry him and simply refuses to take her refusal for an answer, harrying her through the house until Mr. Bennet supports her demurral. Stung by Elizabeth's refusal, Collins then proposes to her good friend Charlotte Lucas, who accepts him in full awareness of his limitations.

The ironies here are many and cutting. The intelligent characters in the book—Mr. Bennet, Elizabeth, and even Charlotte—are on to Collins, yet he ultimately succeeds and prospers. Even this most clumsy and obvious of flatterers flourishes, marrying a wife far beyond his deserts and effectively harnessing her intelligence to his sycophantic ambitions. Elizabeth is left with "the pang of a friend disgracing herself and sunk in her esteem" (125).

Austen depicts more artful flatterers in other novels, flatterers who defy such easy categorization as Mr. Collins. But while the portrait of Collins itself lacks depth, Austen does not fail to register the complexities of the social order in which he moves and finds considerable success. The ironic delight that Mr. Bennet and Elizabeth take in Collins's inane blandishments soon curdles into a hard truth about the effectiveness of flattery. Even so inept a lickspittle as Collins can find favor. So long as there is power— here aristocrats such as Lady Catherine who cultivate and patronize adulators—there is opportunity and reward for those willing to lick the boot.

Sycophancy Triumphant

Dante asks, "how bad?" and Shakespeare asks, "how pervasive?" But for each writer there is some end to sycophancy: for Dante, in eternal damnation; for Shakespeare, perhaps less optimistically, in the tendency of sycophants to destroy each other. Later writers do not envision such comeuppance. In *Sense and Sensibility* (1811), Jane Austen provides a rich account of the utility of sycophancy. Virtue is, as the adage reminds us, its own reward in the polite society of Austen's novel, but sycophancy pays awfully well, too.

Austen's novels are chock-full of sycophants, from the insufferable Mr. Collins in *Pride and Prejudice*, to the ever-excusing Mrs. Norris in *Mansfield Park*, to the cloying Mrs. Clay in *Persua-*

sion. But *Sense and Sensibility* offers the most sustained and most troubling examination of the type. In Lucy Steele, the duplicitous rival to the protagonist, Elinor Dashwood, Austen presents sycophancy triumphant. Miss Steele adroitly silences Elinor through a brilliant campaign of apparent frankness and confession. By revealing her secret engagement to Edward Ferrars, the man Elinor loves, she forces Elinor into a complicity that thwarts her interests and potential happiness.

Austen catalogues Lucy's gushing flattery as she insinuates herself into several families and ultimately jilts her fiancé to elope with his richer brother. The narrator's last remarks on Lucy's relentless sycophancy combine irony with a resignation to such evils. Miss Steele's success is "a most encouraging instance of what an earnest, an unceasing attention to self interest, however its progress may be apparently obstructed, will do in securing every advantage of fortune, with no other sacrifice than of time and conscience."[4] Austen has carefully cultivated a reader who would be sensitive to the ironic force of "encouraging" as well as the exquisite moral sanction implied by putting "time" and "conscience" on equal footing as "sacrifices." The sycophant cannot distinguish the one from the other. But despite the narrator's disapproval, and although her heroine Elinor does marry happily, Lucy nevertheless succeeds in her ambitions. Austen describes an imperfect world, one in which fortune favors those brash and amoral enough to pursue personal interests relentlessly. Repercussions are left to some afterlife.

Austen subscribes to and expands upon Shakespeare's view that sycophancy requires enablers. The relation is thoroughly codependent. Just as Lear enjoins his daughters to compete in professions of sycophancy, so do Austen's characters encourage and nourish sycophancy. Numerous characters are only too ready to acquiesce to Lucy's gross flatteries, and they find her smiling acceptance of unpleasant tasks—such as minding and praising Lady Middleton's unruly children—a convenient and fitting tribute to their position. Lady Middleton and Fanny Dashwood, ever eager for praise, overlook Lucy's lack of polish, information, and morals again and again.

In fact, Austen reinforces this sad lesson about the power of sycophancy in her final chapter. Although Lucy's skills in ingratiation and flattery gain her a marriage beyond any reasonable expectation she might have, her new mother-in-law reviles her. This displeasure constitutes some penalty for Lucy's duplicity and ingratiation. But Austen's narrator assures us that after a campaign of abasement and fawning attention Lucy is forgiven and welcomed into the family. Such is the force of assiduous sycophancy—or, perhaps more exactly, such is the hunger for the kind of comfort that sycophants provide. Mrs. Ferrars eventually finds her cunning daughter-in-law's effusions most acceptable. But, by contrast, she finds little use for her other daughter-in-law, Elinor. As with Kent, Elinor's frankness is seen as obduracy, and her modest, plainspoken, but unfailingly polite truth is unwelcome. As the fool in Lear puts it, "truth's a dog that must to kennel"—that is, it must be managed like a troublesome, noisy pet.

We can gauge the discontent of this deceptively quiet ending by comparing it with that of the 1995 film adaptation, directed by Ang Lee. Emma Thompson's script avoids the bitter testimony of the novel by adding a scene that provides a measure of retribution for the sycophant Lucy. In the film we see Lucy confess her hidden engagement to her future sister-in-law, who attacks her violently. This humiliation, a decidedly un-Austen-like catfight far from the genteel world depicted in the book, allows the audience to feel some relief from Lucy's steady string of triumphs. That Thompson chose to temper what the book terms Lucy's "selfish sagacity" suggests that she is a fine judge of the limits of what a modern audience will endure from a sycophant. The triumph of such a figure cannot be so decisive. And of course, the film rewards Elinor abundantly with the dishy Hugh Grant, a definite upgrade from the virtuous but plodding Edward of the novel. Austen's unpalatable truth here, that sycophancy can succeed spectacularly, "must to kennel" as well.

Charivari Revisited

Sometimes the sheer energy of a depiction of sycophancy seizes us. Charles Dickens does not provide much depth of analysis of the type in his novel *Great Expectations*, but we are swept along by the brio and bustle of the flatterer. The narrator's uncle, Mr. Pumblechook, appears initially as a pompous bore, lecturing his nephew on market forces and laissez-faire economics, recommending abasement-level gratitude toward "them which brought you up by hand," and quizzing him endlessly on the mathematics of converting pounds and shillings and pence. But when Pip becomes heir to a mysterious fortune, the "great expectations" of the novel's title, Pumblechook assumes a very different posture:

> "My dear friend," said Mr. Pumblechook, taking me by both hands, when he and I and the collation were alone, "I give you joy of your good fortune. Well deserved, well deserved."[5]

Dickens distills Pumblechook's hypocritical fawning into a memorable gesture, the essence of good caricature:

> "But do I," said Mr. Pumblechook, getting up again the moment after he had sat down, "see afore me, him as I ever sported with in his times of happy infancy? And may I—*may I*—?"
> This May I, meant might he shake hands? I consented, and he was fervent, and then sat down again. (154)

Pumblechook takes every occasion to repeat this absurd ritual as they share a meal, and Pip luxuriates in this celebration of his "deserved" expectations. Dickens shows little interest in Pumblechook's motivations beyond his obsequious request that Pip might, with the magic application of that great fairy "more capital," realize huge profits as his sleeping partner in the corn-factor business. Dickens instead considers the effect of flattery on Pip, which he likens to the intoxicating effect of the wine the two drink as they share a celebratory meal.

Pip is corrupted almost as soon as he gains his great expectations, and he becomes vulnerable to even the coarsest flatteries. He revels in the new attentions that the local haberdasher lavishes upon him as he orders new clothes, and he rebukes his childhood friend Biddy for her failure to register sufficient wonder at his "rise in station." Pip even faults Joe, the uncle who has protected

"AND MAY I—MAY I—?"

"And may I—may I—?" Pip and Pumblechook. Illustration by John McLenan, *Harper's Weekly*, February 16, 1861, for Charles Dickens, *Great Expectations*. (Courtesy of the Albert and Shirley Small Special Collections, University of Virginia)

and indulged him, for inadequate reverence: "I should have liked him to have betrayed emotion, or to have said, 'It does you credit, Pip,' or something of the sort" (149).

Dickens's treatment of Pip's snobbism comes to a satisfying climax fairly soon in the novel. It takes the form of an ingenious public shaming by Trabb's boy, the haberdasher's helper, a character barely noticed up to this point. Pip has returned home for a visit, and as he walks through the town, his egotism is on full display:

It was not disagreeable to be here and there suddenly recognized and stared after. One or two of the tradespeople even darted out of their shops and went a little way down the street before me, that they might turn, as if they had forgotten something, and pass me face to face. (233)

Pip colludes in this droll little pageant. If the tradespeople pretend not to do what they are doing, so does he pretend not to notice the artifice that obscures their groveling. Client and patron move together in a performance as elaborate as Kabuki theater.

But Trabb's boy bursts the self-satisfied bubble in which Pip and the sycophantic corps of tradesmen float above the demands of life within a cash economy. Sensing trouble as the boy approaches, Pip tries to ignore him. But the other has a plan:

> Suddenly the knees of Trabb's boy smote together, his hair uprose, his cap fell off, he trembled violently in every limb, staggered out into the road, and crying to the populace, "Hold me! I'm so frightened!" feigned to be in a paroxysm of terror and contrition, occasioned by the dignity of my appearance. As I passed him, his teeth loudly chattered in his head, and with every mark of extreme humiliation, he prostrated himself in the dust. (233)

Here caricature becomes charivari—the rough, mock celebration or serenade of a detested person. Trabb's boy's performance is brilliant. By exaggerating Pip's smug expectations of deference, it deftly exposes both sides in the sycophantic exchange—the target as well as the swarm of sycophants that surrounds him. Pip perhaps feels the sting of this spectacle most keenly, but Trabb's boy also exposes the simpering tradesmen who now defer to Pip.

Dickens extends this exposure of the "flatterer within" in a series of repetitions. By looping around the block ahead of Pip as he walks, Trabb's boy is able to give two other performances, each adding new derisive elements—"he staggered round and round me with knees more uplifted, and with uplifted hands as if beseeching for mercy" (233)—that ultimately draw a joyful audience. Then Trabb's boy switches roles, sporting a bag as if it were Pip's greatcoat, and loftily shunning both Pip and passersby:

He pulled up his shirt-collar, twined his side-hair, stuck an arm akimbo, and smirked extravagantly by, wriggling his elbows and body, and drawling to his attendants, "Don't know yah, don't know yah, pon my soul don't know yah." (234)

This bit of street theater delivers a disruptive truth, not only about Pip's fall from innocence but also about the sycophancy fostered by the cash nexus. Trabb's satire derides Pip's inflated sense of self but also the petty flatteries of trade. "Capital," as Pumblechook puts it in hushed tones as he sucks up to Pip, elicits sycophancy just as powerfully as gradations in rank. The charivari, once a weapon of those oppressed within a feudal system, now finds new targets in the new world of capitalism.

State-Sponsored Sycophancy

Austen's novels remind us that sucking up isn't simply a personal failing. Others elicit, encourage, and even require it. In *David Copperfield*, Charles Dickens depicts the most famous of all literary sycophants, a character whose name has become synonymous with a particularly servile and self-serving brand of flattery: Uriah Heep. Finely attuned to the workings of society, Dickens takes care to provide his readers with a rich account of Heep's formation and his perspective. In *David Copperfield*, the depiction of sycophancy takes an inward turn.

Uriah Heep is a formidable sycophant. Beginning with a lowly position as a clerk in Mr. Wickfield's law office, he insinuates his way into control of the firm by aggravating and exploiting his employer's vices and weaknesses. Ultimately, he masters his master through threats and blackmail, strips his clients of their assets, and angles at a marriage with his employer's daughter, Agnes. Heep's malice is endless. He skillfully extracts information from the young David, and he often entraps others in an unwelcome complicity in his schemes. He seems particularly eager to cause marital discord, as he initiates a whispering campaign against a young wife (Annie Strong) and creates a distance between his own clerk and his wife (Mr. and Mrs. Micawber). Only an ingenious campaign of infiltration and a commanding exposure by Micawber bring Uriah Heep to justice. Micawber, acting as clerk to Heep, unmasks the villain, exposing his malice, hypocrisy, and hatred to all. The takedown could not be more spectacular. Uriah is "the most consummate villain that ever existed"—a veritable "HEEP of infamy."[6]

Dickens at once sets Heep apart from other characters in the novel, describing him as "cadaverous," red-haired, and "bony," with a "long, lank, skeletal hand." He refines this initial impression of creepiness by expanding upon Heep's "lank" aspects. Uriah has "damp, fishy fingers," and these repellent qualities coalesce later in descriptions of Heep as a snake or eel. His contortions and writhing convey succinctly his fawning and ingratiation. As David's Aunt Betsy puts it: "If you're an eel, sir, conduct yourself like one. If you're a man, control your limbs, sir! I'm not going to be serpentined and corkscrewed out of my senses" (478).

Heep's flattery knows no bounds. Quick to affirm that he knows and relishes his lowly place, he conspicuously abases himself before young David. Working in concert with his mother, Uriah launches a series of bizarre compliments:

> "This is a day to be remembered, my Uriah, I am sure," said Mrs. Heep, making the tea, "when Master Copperfield pays us a visit." "I said you'd think so, mother," said Uriah. "If I could have wished father to remain among us for any reason," said Mrs. Heep, "it would have been, that he might have known his company this afternoon." (242)

To wish the return of a parent from the grave simply for the purpose of taking tea with a twelve-year-old would certainly register high on any list of flatteries. Years later, when David interviews Heep after his crimes are exposed, the convict will match this sacrifice of his father's memory with an equivalent humiliation of his mother: Heep compliments the warden's correctional methods by wishing that Mrs. Heep could reap the benefits of imprisonment as well.

Unctuous, undulating, and unpleasant—"his hand felt like a

fish in the dark"—Heep is not simply sycophantic. His is a fully weaponized sycophancy by means of which he not only pursues his interests relentlessly but also smears and soils his antagonists. "Humble"—or, as the cocknified Uriah pronounces it, "umble"—is a key word in Dickens's presentation. "Umble" professions of humility form the basis of Heep's conversation. Copperfield's first exchange with Heep is typical:

> "I suppose you are quite a great lawyer?" I said after looking at him for some time. "Me, Master Copperfield?" said Uriah. "Oh, no! I'm a very umble person."
>
> It was no fancy of mine about his hands, I observed; for he frequently ground the palms against each other as if to squeeze them dry and warm, besides often wiping them, in a stealthy way, on his pocket handkerchief. "I am well-aware that I am the umblest person going," said Uriah Heep, modestly; "let the other be where he may. My mother is likewise a very umble person. We live in an umble abode, Master Copperfield, but have much to be thankful for. My father's former calling was umble. He was a sexton." (223)

One might accuse Dickens of excessive repetition here, as "umble" appears in each sentence Heep utters. But Dickens will trace this word's history in Heep's life carefully, and repetition here is less a stylistic tic than a means of aggression.

Unlike Lucy Steele, who has no real past in *Sense and Sensibility*, Heep's history emerges clearly in a series of conversations with David. When Copperfield objects to Heep's "umble" rhetoric, he receives a surprisingly sophisticated reply:

> "But how little you think of the rightful umbleness of a person in my station, Master Copperfield! Father and me was both brought up at a foundation school for boys; and mother, she was likewise brought up at a public, sort of charitable, establishment. They taught us all a deal of umbleness—not much else that I know of, from morning to night. We was to be umble to this person, and umble to that; and to pull off our caps here, and to make bows there; and always to know our place, and abase ourselves

before our betters. And we had such a lot of betters! Father got
the monitor-medal by being umble. So did I. Father got made a
sexton by being umble. He had the character, among the gentle-
folks, of being such a well-behaved man, that they were deter-
mined to bring him in. 'Be umble, Uriah,' says father to me, 'and
you'll get on. It was what was always being dinned into you and
me at the school; it's what goes down best. Be umble,' says father,
'and you'll do!' And really it ain't done bad!"

It was the first time it had ever occurred to me, that this de-
testable cant of false humility might have originated out of the
Heep family. I had seen the harvest, but had never thought of the
seed. (530–31)

The implications of this confession take us far beyond the narrowly self-serving sycophancy of Lucy Steele. Heep launches a
thorough criticism of the society that formed him, exposing its
hypocrisies and registering his own resentments at its shaping
hand. The charitable institutions he attended schooled him in
the arts of ingratiation. Their largess was "umble pie," not kindness; their principles a contradictory mix of evangelical piety and
market ideologies. "People like to be above you," Heep's father advises, and his son makes ingratiation into a weapon against a society bent upon subordinating him. Charity—at least of a certain
kind—produces sycophancy, and the novel's villain becomes an
unexpected truth-teller.

Dickens's genius lies in his ability to move beyond anecdotes
about personalities to the display of social types, which he connects in surprising ways. We last encounter Uriah Heep in prison,
where he has become a model prisoner in a dubious scheme of
reformation. Copperfield's old schoolmaster, the malevolent Mr.
Creakle, has become warden, and he is eager to show off his suc-
cesses in prison reeducation. Heep emerges from his cell with a
characteristic profession of "umbleness," and he brilliantly performs his role as penitent for his visitors. He has come to understand, during his solitary confinement, his "sin," and he deftly
turns his newfound state of humble grace into an instrument of
revenge:

"Oh, thank you, Master Copperfield," said Uriah Heep, "for that remark! It is so true! Umble as I am, I know it is so true! Oh, thank you, Master Copperfield!" Illustration by Fred Barnard, *Scenes and Characters from the Works of Charles Dickens* (n.d.). (Courtesy of the Albert and Shirley Small Special Collections, University of Virginia)

"But I forgive you, Mr. Copperfield," said Uriah, making his forgiving nature the subject of a most impious and awful parallel, which I shall not record. "I forgive everybody. It would ill become me to bear malice. I freely forgive you and I hope you'll curb your passions in future. I hope Mr. W. will repent, and Miss W., and all of that sinful lot. You've been visited with affliction, and I hope it may do you good; but you'd better have come here. Mr. W. had better have come here, and Miss W. too. The best wish I could give you, Mr. Copperfield, and give all of you gentlemen, is, that you could be took up and brought here. When I think of my past follies, and my present state, I am sure it would be best for you. I pity all who ain't brought here!" (785)

Nowhere is Heep's ingenuity, his ability to turn apparent weakness into a weapon, more evident. While mouthing the platitudes required by society, he deftly exposes its hypocrisies and its blindness to the cruelties it carries out in the name of reform. Heep "forgives," but with each act of forgiveness he accuses someone. Similarly, his "pity" amounts to a curse. This penitence is entirely false, a tongue-in-cheek, near-comic performance in which Heep brazenly doubles himself with Christ, wishes incarceration on all the "gentlemen" before him, and manages, by a clever verbal jujitsu, to turn his meekness and humility into a method of debasing others.

The scene has uneasy implications for the reader. Through this slimiest of sycophants, Dickens connects school (through the schoolmaster turned warden) to prison, he spotlights society's harsh insistence on subordination of the lower classes, and he unmasks Christian faith as a will to power. What was implicit in Mr. Collins's confusion of self-interest and religion is here manifest in Heep's deliberate scheming. The sycophant is conscious of his sycophancy, and, more importantly, those who enforce sycophantic behavior bear a responsibility for it.

Wormtongue

Readers have appreciated the force of Uriah Heep, but writers have also paid tribute to Dickens's unctuous creation. J. R. R. Tolkien provides a variation on this figure in *The Lord of the Rings*. Advisor to King Theóden of Rohan and the wizard Saruman's henchman, Gríma Wormtongue exemplifies the destructive effects of sycophancy. Tolkien's very name for this wheedling creature highlights his repulsiveness: Gríma in Old English and Icelandic means "mask," "helmet," or "spectre," thus emphasizing the hypocritical nature of sycophants. "Wormtongue" speaks for itself: as sinuous as the slithering creature whose name he shares, Theóden's insidious advisor wreaks havoc with every word he hisses. His malicious insinuations have poisoned the mind of Theóden, now a shadow of himself. Rohan, once the great kingdom of the Horse-lords, has been reduced to an ineffectual state presided over by a puppet monarch. Like Uriah Heep, who covets his employer's daughter, Agnes Wickfield, Wormtongue desires Eowyn, the king's niece.

When the wizard Gandalf, accompanied by Aragorn, Gimli,

and Legolas, seeks an audience with the king to elicit Rohan's help in fighting Sauron's evil forces, they find themselves before a wizened Theóden, highly skeptical of his claims concerning the Dark Lord. As soon as Theóden expresses his misgivings about Gandalf's claims, Wormtongue, affecting to be protective of the king, sharpens the attack on the wizard and accuses him of being in league with Galadriel, co-leader of Lothlórian, one of the elven kingdoms. Incensed by Wormtongue's slanders, Gandalf sheds his tattered traveling cloak, stands erect, and coldly denounces the servant: "The wise speak only of what they know, Gríma son of Gálmód. A witless worm have you become. Therefore be silent, and keep your forked tongue behind your teeth. I have not passed through fire and death to bandy crooked words with a serving-man till the lightning falls."[7] The hall resounds with a roll of thunder and grows suddenly dark as Gandalf raises his staff, standing tall before the Lord of the Mark and urging him to hearken to his words. Freed from the sycophant's deceptions—Wormtongue's "leechcraft"—Theóden now stands erect, returned to his former self, and ready to take up arms against the enemy.

Tolkien's depiction is notable for its focus on the effects of sycophancy. Wormtongue is not only loathsome in himself, but he engineers the degeneration of his target. Just as Uriah Heep drains and exhausts his pitiable employer, Wormtongue enfeebles Theóden to the point of childishness and isolates him from contact with all others. Once he is freed by Gandalf's magic, his transformation is a measure of the power of sycophancy. So poisonous are its effects that it takes a wizard to banish them.

The servant ultimately turns on his master. After the destruction of the Ring, Saruman and Wormtongue turn their attentions to the Shire. Frodo, Sam, Pippin, Merry, and Gandalf encounter the miserable pair at Bag End. Saruman spitefully informs the hobbits that Wormtongue has killed Lotho, their chief, kicking and taunting his servant as he dishes—"You do what Sharkey says, always, don't you, Worm?"[8] Having groveled for the last time, Wormtongue slits Saruman's throat in a fit of rage. The empowered hobbits then kill Wormtongue. A fitting end for this most loathsome of sycophants.

Few of us will ever encounter as venomous a combination of slander and sycophancy as that found in Wormtongue, a fantasy figure. Nor, alas, are malevolent toadies dispatched so completely in life as in *The Lord of the Rings*. They persist, and they pose a continual challenge to the workings of any hierarchical society.

Sycophancy as
an Art Form

A Place for Flattery

Literature paints a devastating picture of sycophancy, from Milton's conception of flattery as the engine of original sin, to Shakespeare's sycophancy-fueled apocalypse in *King Lear,* to Austen's analysis of its pervasiveness in society, to Dickens's investigation of the state's role in fostering it. We see how difficult it is to distinguish flattery from friendship, how ingenious flatterers can be, how pervasive the practice is, and how effective it can be. These works encourage us to think more abstractly about sycophancy. Everyone can register disgust or sorrow at some personal encounter with a flatterer, but Dante reminds us that there is a social dimension to such dissimulation, that flattery is an assault on the wider community.

We can, given the richness and depth of literature's treatment of sycophancy, simply admire the view, luxuriating in a sense of how well a play like *Othello* reflects life. But we needn't stop there. For a behavior like sycophancy, which is essentially a performance, a drama with prescribed roles (and even a space for an audience), this deep continuity between life and art is especially pronounced. There is something artistic in the self-fashioning of sycophants and flatterers.

Let's now turn to a book that examines the performative nature of sycophancy, Baldassare Castiglione's *Book of the Courtier.* Then, in the next two sections, we'll examine a pair of historical figures—Benjamin Disraeli and Emma Hamilton—who gave their sycophancy artistic form. Finally, we'll look at Tony Blair's performance in the run-up to and aftermath of the Iraq War, in which his intentions—revealed more fully in a recently released document—are overwhelmed by circumstance.

An accomplished diplomat, Baldassare Castiglione (1478–1529) undertook several high-level negotiations during his lifetime, but history remembers him primarily for his graceful portrait of the ideal courtier, published in 1528. *The Book of the Courtier* is cast as a dialogue recorded over four nights at the ducal court in Urbino. Among other refined pastimes, the court pursued various intellectual games, setting topics for discussion that allowed for conspicuous display of eloquence, knowledge, and wit. Guidobaldo da Montefeltro's court, presided over by his wife, Elisabetta Gonzaga, attracted a glittering array of nobles and intellectuals, making it the ideal forum in which to pursue the question of the perfect courtier.

Courts were changing rapidly, and Castiglione's work reflects this transformation. *The Book of the Courtier* imagines the ideal courtier as a warrior first and foremost, but Castiglione adds a host of other requirements. He must be knowledgeable in Latin and Greek, music, dancing, and painting, but he must carry these accomplishments lightly, with *sprezzatura*—a certain nonchalance.

The first speaker in *The Book of the Courtier*, Count Ludovico da Canossa, provides a recognizable portrait of the Renaissance man, that dazzling combination of erudition, tact, and martial prowess. The second speaker, Federico Fregoso, reminds his listeners that these qualities are not pursued simply for themselves:

> I would have the Courtier devote all his thought and strength of spirit to loving and almost adoring the prince he serves above all else, devoting his every desire and habit and manner to pleasing him.[1]

This prompts a quick response from one of Fregoso's listeners, who sarcastically notes that there are many such courtiers in Italian courts, "for it strikes me that you have, in few words, sketched us a noble flatterer" (80).

Here we are again. Just as telling friend from flatterer pro-
vokes anxiety in Plutarch's essay, so does telling courtier from
sycophant perplex Castiglione's elegant speakers. Behavior in itself cannot settle this. Fregoso defends himself with considerable
hedging:

> Flatterers love neither their prince nor their friends, which I wish
> our Courtier to do above all else; and it is possible to obey and
> to further the wishes of the one he serves without adulation, be-
> cause by wishes I mean such as are reasonable and right, or those
> which in themselves are neither good nor bad. (80–81)

Note the uneasy steps Fregoso takes in his response. Avoiding
adulation is "possible." Compliance in things "neither good nor
bad" is not, according to Fregoso, sycophancy. Fregoso's eventual
return to describing the ideal courtier focuses on the courtier's
ability to make himself small. He advises the courtier to avoid
presumption, ask little from his lord, make amusing small talk
when alone with him, and be humble. Such behaviors seem, well,
sycophantic.

This grumbling exchange, for all its courtly elegance, seems
quite modern. Other courtiers, insisting upon their own experience, contradict Fregoso's portrait of modest duty finding its
reward from wise and appreciative princes. When Fregoso specifically prohibits the kind of sycophancy that others feel is routine
in courts, contending that a courtier should "be neither envious
nor evil tongued; nor let him ever bring himself to seek grace or
favor by resorting to foul means or evil practices" (85), Calmeta
assures him that such behaviors not only pervade life in courts
but are far more effective than modesty and honesty. Cornered,
Fregoso argues that no courtier need follow a prince who encour-
ages sycophancy and flattery:

> But if our Courtier happens to find himself in the service of one
> who is wicked and malign, let him leave him as soon as he discov-
> ers this, that he may escape the great anguish that all good men
> feel in serving the wicked. (85)

Calmeta's reply would resonate to many in today's workplaces, where mobility is often limited and especially difficult when suddenly necessary. With some weariness, Calmeta points to "countless considerations" that "force a gentleman not to leave a patron once he has begun to serve him" (85), and he dolorously notes that the misfortune of a bad employer leaves courtiers "like those unhappy birds that are born in some miserable valley" (85).

The "countless considerations" that bind one to a terrible job have changed over time, but Calmeta's lament is familiar. Fregoso's reply, that one "ought to quit" a bad prince, seems unrealistic. Castiglione's perfect courtier is met at every turn by an imperfect world, one infested with willing sycophants and leaders all too ready to be flattered and to prefer flattery.

Sycophancy shadows honest service throughout *The Book of the Courtier*, in the same way that flattery and friendship are entangled in Plutarch. During the final night of discussion, the courtiers again turn from the courtier's accomplishments themselves to the reason for developing such skills. Perfection as a courtier is defined by doing, not simply being. Ottaviano Fregoso amplifies his brother Federico's statements:

> Therefore, I think that the aim of the perfect Courtier, which we have not spoken of up to now, is so to win for himself, by means of the accomplishments ascribed to him by these gentlemen, the favor and mind of the prince whom he serves that he may be able to tell him, and always will tell him, the truth about everything he needs to know. (210)

Although none present pose the earlier objection, that the means to this end seem indistinguishable from the behavior of a "noble flatterer," readers of *The Book of the Courtier* cannot fail to recall it. The ability of the courtier to "adapt himself to the occasion" (77), to amuse his patron with small talk, to bend to his preferences in indifferent things, and to put his learning and wit on display has an ultimate purpose. The "favor acquired by his good accomplishments" (210) allows the courtier to oppose a prince who falls into error or strays from virtue.

In other words, the courtier's flatteries are redeemed by later action—moments of decisive intervention when the courtier gives unwelcome but necessary advice. As in Plutarch's essay, the behavior takes meaning from the aim behind it, and, as the more worldly courtiers in Castiglione remind us, that aim is often difficult to discern. But truth is also enabled by flattery. Truth is a precious stone made lovely by the foil of a thousand little attendant blandishments.

The Sycophantic Sublime: Benjamin Disraeli

We can trace the entanglement of friendship and flattery that haunts *The Book of the Courtier* in the career of Benjamin Disraeli (1804–1881), who famously told the poet Matthew Arnold: "You have heard me called a flatterer and it is true. Everyone likes flattery, and when you come to Royalty you should lay it on with a trowel."[2] In person and through his letters Disraeli spun a gossamer romance around Queen Victoria, the ruler he frequently referred to as the Faery, a tribute adapted from *The Faerie Queene*, Edmund Spenser's epic poem dedicated to Elizabeth I.

Posterity has deemed Disraeli one of the most exceptional public figures of British history. Disraeli could not have been more different from his political colleagues. He was the first and is to date the only Jewish prime minister of England. Self-educated from the age of fifteen, he never attended public school or university. He was a flamboyant dandy. Imbued from youth with an ardent desire to be remarkable and fired by the exploits of his hero, the Romantic poet Byron, Disraeli first gained fame as a writer, largely of social and political novels, and then as a politician for the Conservative Party. Once he entered the House of Commons in 1837, his exceptional oratorical skills, masterly command of parliamentary procedure, and bold self-presentation made him a star of his party. Disraeli didn't just deliver speeches; he performed them. Oscar Wilde, neatly balancing Disraeli's range of talent and dexterity, wrote that he was a "man who could write a novel and govern an empire with either hand."[3] The Liberal Party was dominant during most of Disraeli's career. He was prime minister briefly in 1868 and returned to power in 1874–80.

Part of governing Britain in the nineteenth century meant carefully maintaining one's relations with the ruling monarch, Victoria. The transfer of power between feudal and democratic structures was steady, but tradition and sentiment made the queen a force to reckon with in practice. Disraeli took a somewhat novel tone toward Victoria, that of sycophantic admirer. Disraeli's letters to his "Sovereign Mistress" abound with grace notes. The letter he wrote the queen upon his second appointment sets the tone of their correspondence until his death in 1881:

> Mr. Disraeli with his humble duty to Your Majesty.
>
> He ventures to express his sense of your Majesty's most gracious kindness to him, and of the high honour which your Majesty has been graciously pleased to confer on him.
>
> He can only offer devotion.
>
> It will be his delight and duty to render the transaction of affairs as easy to your Majesty as possible; and in smaller matters he hopes he may succeed in this; but he ventures to trust that, in the great affairs of state, your Majesty will deign not to withhold from him the benefit of your Majesty's guidance.
>
> Your Majesty's life has been passed in constant communication with great men, and the knowledge and management of important transactions. Even if your Majesty were not gifted with those great abilities, which all now acknowledge, this rare and choice experience must give your Majesty an advantage in judgment which few living persons, and probably no living prince, can rival.
>
> He whom your Majesty has so highly preferred presumes to trust to your Majesty's condescension in this behalf.[4]

Disraeli assumes a complicated rhetorical stance. The romance begins as he pays tribute to the queen's "rare and choice" experience and presents himself as the honored beneficiary of her gracious condescension. Yet, as the prime minister himself liked to put it, he never forgot that the queen was a woman. He imbued their exchanges with a chivalric ardor artfully designed to assure her of his fidelity and gain her sympathy. Victoria took pleasure in Disraeli's boundless proclamations of personal devotion, all the more because she felt that William Gladstone, Disraeli's rival and leader of the Liberal Party, had always addressed her as if she were a "public meeting."[5] Disraeli's gifts as raconteur—his sparkling accounts of society and political meetings—gave her the impression that she was his confidante in all matters of state. As a lady-in-waiting revealed to Lord Clarendon, one of the Whigs, "She declares that she has never had such letters in her life, which is probably true, and that she never before knew *everything*."[6]

Disraeli was quick to lay every one of his greatest political and diplomatic triumphs at the feet of Victoria—at least rhetorically. After the acquisition of the khedive of Egypt's 44 percent share of the Suez Canal, Disraeli wrote: "It is just settled: you have it, Madam. The French Government has been out-generaled . . . the entire interest of the Khedive is now yours."[7] Notwithstanding the disapproval of many Liberals and some Conservatives at such dramatic accounts, which they feared would heighten the queen's sense of her own power, Disraeli's obeisance never waned. Until his last letters he never failed to underscore "how deeply and finely he feels the privilege of being the trusted servant of a Sovereign whom he adores!"[8] Disraeli's politics—an imaginative mixture of reactionary and feudal ideologies—had served him well in fiery backbench speeches early in his career, when he excoriated the economic programs of the Liberals. Here his politics again opened a space in which a picturesque nostalgia could be deployed forcefully. As the power of the aristocracy and the crown waned, Disraeli's call to earlier times—to knight errantry and gallantry—evoked a familiar tale.

The two exchanged gifts: he gave Victoria copies of his books, and she sent him flowers. These floral gifts never failed to elicit florid notes of thanks from her devoted knight. Upon receiving some primroses from Osborne, the queen's estate on the Isle of Wight, Disraeli fancifully compares himself to the nymph Proserpine, whose return to earth every six months from Hades signals the arrival of spring. The primroses remind him "that there might yet be spring & tho' Proserpine be absent there is happily for him a Queen to whom he is devoted at Windsor."[9] While one might fault the pernicious tendencies of such correspondence, which, after all, serves to personalize great matters of state and inflate the queen's sense of her centrality to the nation, one cannot but admire the daring in Disraeli's missives. After a banquet at which he had seen many heads of state festooned in medallions and assorted gewgaws, he wrote one of his most extravagant effusions:

> Yesterday eve, there appeared . . . a delicate looking case, with a royal inscription which, when he opened, he thought, at first, that your Majesty had graciously bestowed upon him the stars of your Majesty's principal orders. And, indeed, he was so impressed with this graceful illusion, that, having a banquet, where there were many stars and ribbons, he could not resist the temptation, by placing some snowdrops on his heart, of showing that he, too, was decorated by a gracious Sovereign.
>
> Then in the middle of the night, it occurred to him, that it might be an enchantment, and that, perhaps, it was a Faery gift and came from another monarch: Queen Titania gathering flowers with her Court, in a soft and sea-girt isle, and sending magic blossoms which, they say, turn the heads of those who receive them.
>
> They certainly would turn Mr. Disraeli's head, if his sense of duty to your Majesty did not exceed, he sincerely believes, his conceit.[10]

Disraeli's rhetoric here soars to the outer edges of the galaxy and the outer limits of plausibility. This is flattery at its most sublime. Sublimation, we should recall, is a chemical process that describes the transformation of a solid to a gaseous state. Sycophancy has often been exaggerated but never perhaps become so rarefied. And it worked. What he sought from his target, he often got. The queen lent her support to Disraeli's positions. By the same token, he fulfilled some of the queen's requests—for example, obtaining for her the title of "Empress of India" in the Royal Titles Act in 1876. In the same year she raised him to the peerage as Lord Bea-

"Empress and Earl; or, One Good Turn Deserves Another."
Illustration by John Tenniel, *Punch*, August 28, 1876. (Courtesy of the Albert
and Shirley Small Special Collections, University of Virginia)

consfield. But theirs was more than a simple relation of quid pro quo; it was a game relished by both, a series of mutually flattering dramatic set pieces.

What are we to make of Disraeli's effusions? One could, as some biographers have, conclude that he was an opportunistic adventurer. Sycophancy, as we've seen from Plutarch, is entangled with friendship. Usually sycophants pretend to be friends. But in Disraeli's case we have an example of a friend acting like a sycophant. In his flattering treatment of the queen, Disraeli has effectively reversed the polarities of sycophancy. He could have confined himself to summarizing affairs of state for her like his predecessors. However puckish the letter quoted above, with its gossamer *Midsummer Night's Dream* fairy machinery, few would see Victoria—a short, stout, middle-aged mother of nine—as a fairy, nor Disraeli, a droll urban sophisticate, as gallant knight. Having once famously remarked that he had "climbed to the top of the greasy pole" of political power, the prime minister was clearly under no illusions regarding what it took to get there.

Let's consider again Disraeli's observation to Arnold that "everyone likes flattery, and when you come to Royalty you should lay it on with a trowel." The metaphor here refers to masonry— one uses a trowel to apply mortar or plaster—but it's never clear what kind of edifice Disraeli was constructing. As Victoria revealed to her eldest daughter, in Disraeli she found a prime minister "full of poetry, romance and chivalry."[11] The two were willing participants in a masque that he created for her delectation.

In turn, he won abiding attachment and affection. Upon learning of his death, the queen wrote Lord Rowton, Disraeli's devoted secretary:

> I cannot write in the 3rd person at this terrible moment when I can scarcely see for my fast falling tears. I did *not* expect this very rapid end tho' my hopes sank yesterday very much. . . .
>
> I hardly dare trust to speak of myself. The loss is *so overwhelming. Just a year ago* he came to see me *before* his resignation took place and *then* when I suffered and also at Baden at the thought of losing him as my Minister—and how *he* felt this separation. . . . Never had I *so* kind and devoted a Minister and very few such devoted friends. His affectionate sympathy, his wise counsel—*all* were so invaluable even out of office. I have lost *so* many dear and valued friends but none whose loss will be more keenly felt. To England (or rather Gt. Britain) and to the *World* his loss is *immense* and at such a moment. God's will be done! I have learned to say this but the bitterness and the suffering are not the less severe. As yet I cannot realize it.[12]

Amid these sentiments, one might note the inclusion of a memory of Disraeli's own feeling. The queen recalls the fall of Disraeli's ministry, but only to remark on how he must have felt the ensuing loss of their courtly exchanges. In this exceptional instance the lines of friendship and sycophancy have blurred as those between life and fiction. Disraeli's flatteries are airy confections—sycophancy, perhaps, without slime.

Sycophancy and Self-Fashioning: Emma Hamilton

Disraeli blurs the distinction between "notable flatterer" and faithful advisor. We do not so much judge him as his performance—a performance that he himself ironizes in his comments on it. One can easily imagine Disraeli, called to account by Castiglione's courtiers, nimbly confounding them. Other sycophants seek to redeem their sycophancy through a kind of intensity. Consider the life of Emma, Lady Hamilton (1765–1815). The daughter of a blacksmith, young Amy Lyon rose from squalid poverty to become the wife of Sir William Hamilton, England's envoy to Naples; the muse of the painter George Romney; and the lover of Horatio Lord Nelson, one of the great heroes of the Napoleonic wars. Her story is as fantastical as an Eastern fable. But instead of a genie granting one's wildest wishes, the means of transformation here is sycophancy.

Amy Lyon's ascent to Lady Hamilton, from serving girl to actress's maid to tavern girl to quack doctor's assistant to prostitute to artist's model to the wife of Lord Hamilton in 1791, seems as random as it was steep. What cannot be underestimated is how each of these roles furnished Emma with the skills that would enable her to attract the admiration of royalty and artists. Seemingly nothing was lost on young Amy. As an actress's maid, by which time she had changed her name to Emma Hart, she learned the language of dramatic love from watching theatrical performances, as well as how to cater to the whims of demanding divas—skills that served her well years later when she doted on the queen of Naples. During her brief stint as a prostitute for Madame Kelly, the manager of an exclusive London brothel, Emma learned how to be an ecstatic lover, swooning and crying as the situation required. As a "Goddess of Health" (a term coined by another employer, the self-styled therapist James Graham, whose

Temple of Health featured a "Celestial Bed," a gimmick concocted to help infertile couples through the transmission of mild electrical shocks), Emma learned to dance and strike fetching poses as she and the other "goddesses" paraded about the bed of her clients during the so-called treatments.

She honed her posing skills further while working as a model for the society artist George Romney, who painted Emma more than sixty times in a broad array of allegorical and mythological guises. In *Sensibility,* one of Romney's most popular paintings of Emma, she embodies her favorite poem, William Haley's "The Triumph of Temper," which celebrates the heroine's "wish to please." One would be hard-pressed to imagine a more striking convergence between subject and model.

Finally, as the mistress of the Honorable Charles Greville and later his uncle, William Hamilton, Emma acquired sophistication and discretion, improving herself through reading and singing lessons, learning to dress elegantly, and comporting herself more modestly. Beautiful, pliant, and affectionate, Emma by now excelled in captivation. One could say she lived a charmed life from the moment she became Greville's mistress, but that would be to underestimate her relentless application of flattery and blandishment. As she effused to Greville in a letter, "All my happiness is Greville, & to think that he loves me makes a recompense for all," as she promises to be "gentle affectionate & everything you wishe me to do I will do. . . . I shall think myself happy to be under the same roof with Greville."[13] Hanging on her lover's every word, beseeching his opinions on everything, promising to fulfill all his wishes, Emma was sycophancy incarnate—effusive, compliant, and obedient. Few courtiers or courtesans manage to blend art and nature so energetically and so completely.

By the time Greville had pawned off the twenty-one-year-old on his uncle, who was stationed in Naples, Emma had turned her modeling skills into her famous Attitudes, a kind of performance art in which she mimed theatrical and ancient heroines such as Cleopatra, Dido, and Circe through the artful manipulation of gestures and shawls. The German Romantic poet Goethe, writing in 1787, rhapsodized about her performances: "With a few shawls

[she] gives so much variety to her poses, gestures, expressions etc., that the spectator can hardly believe his eyes. . . . This much is certain: as a performance it is like nothing you ever saw before in your life" (142). Aided and abetted by Lord Hamilton, who saw in Emma the living embodiment of the graceful antique sculptures he collected, Emma rapidly became one of the most famous women in Europe and, in fact, a kind of tourist attraction for well-connected travelers to Naples. The Grand Tour has always featured various Greco-Roman antiquities—buildings, vases, statuary—but the vibrant young Emma seemed to bring the classical past to life. She embodied the beauty of Helen of Troy, the wiles of Circe, and the flatteries of Thaïs as the occasion demanded.

Later the copyist became the copied. Lord William's villa in Naples included fourteen portraits of Emma, not posing as mythological figures but as herself—or the self she had fashioned. Scores of women sought to emulate the nymph-like apparel she wore in Romney's portraits—white, draped gowns modeled on Greek styles with no stays or corsets. Years later the Emma costume included the Maltese cross bestowed upon her by Maria Carolina of Naples ("the Queen whom I adore"), the sister of Marie Antoinette and the queen of Naples. In addition to Romney, Joshua Reynolds, Thomas Lawrence, Gavin Hamilton, Angelica Kaufmann, and Marie-Louise–Elisabeth Vigée le Brun all sought to paint the captivating Emma. Enchanted by her expressive singing, Josef Haydn, the court musician of Prince Esterházy of Vienna, practiced songs with her when he visited Naples. European and British aristocrats clamored to see her Attitudes. Greville once told Sir William that "Emma's passion is admiration" (118).

When Admiral Nelson arrived in Naples in 1798 to convalesce after the Battle of the Nile, Emma leapt at the opportunity to refine her art of ingratiation. She had made the most of her chances in society and in the worlds of art and theater, but now the possibility of fusing sycophancy and patriotic feeling lay before her. England's national life—its existential struggle with Napoleon—was epitomized by Nelson's victory on the Nile. Pulling out all the stops, she sent the victor an epistolary rhapsody before his arrival:

How shall I begin, what shall I say to you 'tis impossible I can write. . . . I am delirious with joy, and assure you I have a fervour caused by agitation and pleasure. God, what a victory! Never, never has there been anything half so glorious, so compleat. I fainted when I heard the joyfull news, and fell on my side am so hurt, but well of that. I shou'd feil it a glory to die in such a cause. No I wou'd not like to die till I see and embrace the Victor of the Nile. How shall I describe to you the transports of Maria Carolina [Queen of Naples], 'tis not possible. She fainted and kissed her husband, her children, walked about the room, cried, kissed and embraced every person near her, exclaiming Oh brave Nelson, oh God bless and protect our brave deliverer, Oh Nelson, Nelson what do we not owe to you, o Victor, Savior of Itali, that my swollen heart cou'd now tell him personally what we owe to him!

The Neapolitans are mad with joy, and if you wos here now, you wou'd be killed with kindness. Sonets on sonnets, illuminations, rejoicings; not a French dog dare shew his face. How I glory in the honor of my Country and my Countryman! I walk and tread in the air with pride, feiling I was born in the same land with the victor Nelson and his gallant band. . . .

My dress from head to foot is alla Nelson. . . . Even my shawl is in Blue with gold anchors all over. I send you some Sonets. . . . I am afraid you will not be able to read this scrawl. (208)

Such ecstatic declarations remind us of how little delicacy is required to be a successful flatterer, if the subject is susceptible. Lay it on and lay it on thick. This is less Disraeli's trowel than a water cannon of admiration, enthusiasm, and adoration. Upon Nelson's arrival in Naples, Emma enacted spectacularly what she had penned, throwing herself at him, crying over his injuries, and fainting against him. An ecstatic Nelson reported to his wife, "Up flew her ladyship . . . and exclaiming 'Oh God is it possible' fell into my arms more dead than alive" (209). Such was his transport that he forgot he had only one arm.

Emma's confession that she was fully decked out "from head to foot alla Nelson" was but the beginning of her campaign to glorify Nelson and her relationship to him. She deftly transformed herself into a living tribute—attending an opera in Naples with two of his captains wearing a headband emblazoned with "Nelson" and "Victory." For Nelson's fortieth birthday party, she invited more than a thousand guests to Hamilton's villa, where adulatory décor was on full display: *Veni, vidi, vici* was inscribed on a column; Nelson's face appeared on every button and ribbon; one of the guests composed a new verse to "God Save the King," which began "Join we great Nelson's name / First on the roll of fame" (212). When Nelson and the Hamiltons returned to England in 1800, "alla Nelson" had become a road show in which Emma always appeared fully decked out in Nelsonian garb, her dress and accessories festooned with anchors and Ns. The Nelsonorama had begun.

With the death of Sir William in 1803, Emma—who had for some time been Nelson's mistress—was free to devote herself wholly to him. The British had, since Nelson's victory, developed an insatiable appetite for patriotic memorabilia, and Nelson gewgaws abounded—pomade boxes, fans, dishes, tea sets, towels. Emma drew these tchotchkes into dress order, constructing the ultimate kitsch monument to Nelson at Merton, where the couple resided from 1801 until Nelson's death. As described by Lord Minto, ex-envoy to Vienna, this gaudy tribute encompassed "not only the rooms, but the whole house, staircase and all, [which] are covered with nothing but pictures of her and him, of all sizes and stores, and representations of his naval actions, coats of arms, pieces of plate in his honour, the flagstaff of L'Orient [one of his ships]." Emma transformed the house into a "mere looking-glass" for Nelson, Minto added, "to view himself all day" (283). Nothing reflected the admiral's accomplishments more brilliantly than his mistress's adoring gaze. Ever adept at serving others, Emma never failed to put on a show with Nelson, serving his food for him in public and trimming his fingernails and toenails in private. Rather spitefully, Minto went on to note that Emma was always "cramming Nelson with trowelfuls of flattery, which he goes on taking as quietly as a child does pap" (289).

Nelson's death at Trafalgar put an end to this domestic extravaganza. The public may have tolerated Emma while Nelson was alive, but as soon as he died it was happy to dismiss her. The

English government showed little interest in honoring Nelson's wish that she be maintained in the event of his death. She wasn't allowed to attend his funeral due to her notoriety; later she was arrested for insolvency and spent a year in debtor's prison. She died abroad, poor and alcoholic.

Nevertheless, while she lived, Emma Hamilton indulged in sycophancy of a rare order and seemed to revel frankly in its performance. She may have begun in the smaller world of mimicry and personal service, but she very soon expanded her repertoire along with her circle of influence. She sought ever-wider stages for her adulation, until, lighting upon her ultimate target, Nelson, she achieved a national prominence. Drawing upon the fine arts, Emma was like a bubble that formed, expanded, and floated aloft. Then, upon her lover's death, the bubble burst, and Emma, Lady Hamilton, disappeared completely.

A Modern Instance: Tony Blair

Moralists might see justice in Emma's fall—a proper ending for an inveterate flatterer. But, like her dramatic posing or the artful drapery of her scarves, her enthralling embodiment of gratitude dazzled Nelson and even the nation for a time. Surely the man whose leadership at the Battle of the Nile had saved the nation deserved such treatment, and his decisive victory at Trafalgar might seem to redeem Emma's adulation as well. Similarly, Disraeli's sycophancy seemed to approach Plutarch's ideal of classical friendship, a relation in which the minister could be trusted to inform and guide the monarch. We might term these cases tolerable sycophancy. But such stratagems can go profoundly wrong, as the experience of Tony Blair amply demonstrates.

During Blair's first few years as prime minister, he was widely admired at home and abroad as a thoughtful, well-informed leader. Eloquent and youthful, he seemed poised to lead Britain into the new century. But his concept of the "special relationship" between Britain and the United States gave many of his countrymen pause. His deference to American interests was a bit too ready, a bit too eager. After 9/11, Blair went all in, becoming a reliable second to George W. Bush's policies. Accordingly he was widely derided in the British press as Bush's "lapdog" (or, in a bit of satire aimed at his notably well-styled hair, a "poodle").

This meme launched scores of cartoons, and it concretized long-standing British anxieties about the nation's relationship with its upstart former colony. Blair persisted, vouching for the Bush administration's dubious claims about weapons of mass destruction in Iraq and repeating many of their talking points in the run-up to the invasion. The catastrophic failure of Bush's policies made Blair's career as yes-man seem even more reprehensible. At the 2006 G-8 summit, Bush inadvertently humiliated Blair with remarks caught on an open microphone. His "Yo, Blair" seemed to encapsulate the prime minister's subservience and his status as convenient dupe. Blair's star dimmed quickly, as members of his own party accused him of misleading them and the nation about the Iraq War, and he resigned in 2007, a greatly diminished figure.

Recently declassified documents both confirm and clarify Blair's attitude toward Bush during the run-up to the war. The July 28, 2002, "Note on Iraq," a personal communication from prime minister to president, shows the limits of the transactional conception of ingratiation. The note begins with an indisputable verification of Blair's sycophancy. In words to make any Briton cringe, Blair writes, "I will be with you, whatever." However, this is followed by six pages of consideration and analysis, much of which astutely predicts the catastrophic failure of the invasion. Clearly Blair sought, as the courtier Fregoso advised, to comply on smaller or indifferent matters in order to gain influence on later, more important decisions. Blair seems to have concluded that he could guide Bush—and presumably the immense military power at his disposal—in beneficial ways. Compliance would be redeemed by true service—not so much to Bush as to the world.

Bush, however, sure of Blair's support, seems to have dismissed the prime minister's cautions completely, driving the United States and its allies headlong into a ruinous war. The rejoinder that Fregoso endured—that such rationalizations for flattery do not change the essentially distasteful nature of the behavior— applies here. Whatever Blair thought he might achieve as lapdog, he remains a "notable flatterer."

Sycophancy on the Silver Screen

Sycophancy Close-Up

We can only imagine Emma Hamilton's acting skills or Disraeli's subtle manipulation of Victoria, but movies allow another kind of access. The immediacy of film—especially classic Hollywood film, with its giant close-ups, speed of development, and rapid cuts among sycophant, target, and bystander—can offer viewers a vivid, near-live experience of sycophancy in action. If novels give us a complex understanding of motives and consequences, movies give us a complex account of the mechanics and techniques of sucking up. Their gorgeous surfaces are especially useful in the study of a practice that relies upon an arsenal of finely honed devices of fraud, hypocrisy, and trickery. The big screen displays sycophancy with microscopic precision.

Almost any discussion of sycophancy, whether a chat among coworkers or the technical descriptions of sociologists, uses theatrical language. Who better, then, than theater folk to understand flattery as performance? Sucking up, stripped to its essentials, is essentially a dramatic performance for an audience of one—the target. And who better than those in the movie business, a sector notorious for the most outrageous kinds of sycophancy, to explore the personal costs of such behavior?

Joseph L. Mankiewicz's 1950 *All about Eve* provides a sharply drawn portrait of an aspiring actress, one whose grand success on the stage cannot match the brilliance of the private performances she gives in order to get her first big part.

Viewers often remember *All about Eve* for Bette Davis's memorable portrayal of Margo Channing, a temperamental actress whose volatility is increased by her fear of aging. Every inch a star, Margo deliberately conflates her personal and professional lives. Apprehensive about her younger lover's fidelity, she plays the tragic heroine at his birthday party, warning anyone who cares to listen to "fasten your seatbelts—it's going to be a bumpy night" as she downs another cocktail. Her anxieties and turbulence finally drive her lover away in a scene played out, fittingly, on her late arrival to a rehearsal: he exits, as she lies facedown in bed center stage.

But if Margo dramatizes everyday life by living it through the oversized gestures and hyperbolic emotions of the theater, her conniving worshiper, Eve Harrington, plays the more exceptional role. Margo imposes on her audience of friends and lovers—one long familiar with her excesses and somewhat tolerant of them—because she acts from a position of power. Eve's performance will be judged more harshly because she has no standing in the theater of her ambitions. Margo acts from a well-known script, one all too familiar to those around her. Eve must brilliantly improvise, and she must bring down the house at every turn. As such, Eve provides a master class in flattery, and *All about Eve* becomes a master text in the study of the connection between sycophancy and performance.

Eve Harrington's commitment to her role as flatterer is total. We first see her standing outside the stage door, as she has for each and every one of Margo Channing's performances, waiting for a glimpse of her idol. A friend of Margo notices her and, approving her apparently starstruck adulation, brings her to meet the great actress in her dressing room. Hidden in her hat and overcoat, Eve plays the dewy-eyed fan, painfully backward, yet, when prompted, wonderfully effective in her earnest praise. Even so plain a line as her opening one, "I like anything Miss Channing played in," proves her powers as an actress. If she can make this banality walk, Broadway should be little challenge for her.

Mankiewicz shrewdly counterpoints Eve's seemingly guileless professions of adoration with a raffishly skeptical crowd of theater people, among them Margo's director boyfriend, Bill; her play's author, Lloyd; and her maid, Birdie. As Eve is coaxed to tell her story, or, more aptly, allowed to read for the part of sycophant, their cynicism seems blunted by her halting but honest-to-goodness account. Initially stumbling—"If I only knew how"—Eve weaves a compelling account of her life. A farmer's daughter with a love of playing at "make-believe," she moves to the big city, where she works in a brewery until she meets and marries "Eddie," a flyboy. Arriving in San Francisco to meet Eddie, who is on leave, she learns of his death in battle. Distraught, Eve happens upon a play in which Margo appears, and she follows her idol to New York City, where she attends every performance. Eve certainly seems to have learned a great deal. This backstage performance, which enthralls the embittered cynics who listen, easily trumps Margo's current role. Only Birdie (played by Thelma Ritter in another of her wonderful wisecracking supporting roles) seems immune to Eve's dramatic prowess. "What a story!" she says dismissively, only to be dismissed in turn by the sophisticates in the audience.

Eve is pitch-perfect and prompt to rise to the occasion, and her career as sycophant accelerates as she becomes Margo's supercompetent girl Friday. Mankiewicz then traces Eve's spectacular trajectory to overnight sensation against her unmasking as a scheming flatterer. Eve marshals the initial feelings of protectiveness she inspires to become Margo's understudy. Even her body language, a slight lean forward as she speaks, expresses her devotion to Margo and her submission to others. As she progresses, however, she must assume other postures. After her initial success, as an opportunistic stand-in when Margo is unable to appear for a performance, she turns her flattery toward Margo's lover, Bill, whom she tries to seduce backstage. For the first time, the audience sees her ability to assume different parts. Her anger at Bill's curt refusal shows her in yet another role, showing Margo-like rage as she tears violently at her hairpiece. But then, as another possible object of flattery—the drama critic Addison DeWitt—enters her dressing room, she must adopt a submissive stance. If Bette Davis has her star turns, as her Margo moves from fury to melodramatic self-pity to acceptance of the inevitability of giving up the spotlight, so too does Anne Baxter's Eve, who combines groveling sycophancy with ruthless manipulation to achieve what producer Darryl Zanuck called "bitch virtuosity."

A scene late in the movie shows the panoply of skills that the virtuoso flatterer must possess. Eve, pretending to be mortified by Margo's anger at an interview she's given that criticizes the practice of casting older actors (like Margo) in parts written for young women (like her), begs Margo's friend Karen to meet her. Adopting her initial role as innocent, she searches for the proper approach to further her career. When stymied, she transforms her entire demeanor at once, bullying Karen with blackmail. This lightning attack, in which the flatterer reveals herself to be a vile schemer, leaves her audience of one dumbfounded and defeated. In a string of performances in which consummate skill, tolerance of risk, and opportunism are all required, Eve has yet again, in theater lingo, "killed."

Ultimately, the plot arrives at a confrontation between the critic DeWitt, a cynic who blends contempt for humankind and insatiable ambition, and Eve, whose career he has promoted. De-Witt's admiration for Eve is almost clinical: "There never was and there never will be another like you," he tells her, as he claims her not just as his discovery but as his creature. Mankiewicz's script makes their likeness clear: Eve's sycophancy is revealed as a will to power, a guise that can now be doffed in the bright light of her success. DeWitt has found out "all about Eve," that her riveting story of starstruck adulation was an opportunistic lie, that her past is checkered with failed plots. He proposes that they speak "killer to killer," and he asserts his new control over her prospects. Mankiewicz intensifies the scene, yet again, by staging it against the overarching frame of the theater. Eve, desolate at DeWitt's power over her, says she cannot go on. DeWitt, however, insists that she will not only perform but that she'll also give the performance of her life. The role-playing of sycophancy has served her well, and she emerges into the limelight.

Mankiewicz's script and direction provide the basis for a profound examination of sucking up. One might note that references to the stage plays in *All about Eve* are limited and satirical: Margo Channing's current triumph seems to be as the lead in some stale southern costume drama. The film's real attention is reserved for the much more demanding performance of sycophancy.

All about Eve began at an awards ceremony, where Eve was

about to receive the highest honor for the Broadway season. After we learn, in a series of flashbacks, all about Eve, we return to this ceremony. There Eve again plays the role of sycophant, accepting her award with thanks to all those whom she flattered and betrayed. Her audience has expanded beyond these few, and her blandishments expand accordingly, to the larger but more impersonal audience of her public. Sycophancy works, it seems.

But Mankiewicz's script takes yet another turn, as Eve returns home alone to find that a young admirer has slipped into her apartment, one just as eager to flatter and serve her idol as she had been with Margo Channing. The movie concludes with this young sycophant, who admires herself in a three-way mirror dressed in Eve's coat and holding her award. Her image reflects not simply three times in the mirror—Mankiewicz provides a shot that multiplies her to infinity. Individual sycophants may rise and fall, but sycophancy, triumphant and ubiquitous, abides.

"A Cookie Laced with Arsenic"

The closer we look at sycophancy in film, the more we find in its merciless close-ups. Alexander Mackendrick's 1957 *Sweet Smell of Success* presents another finely grained portrait of sucking up. Stars Tony Curtis and Burt Lancaster play, respectively, a press agent and a Walter Winchell–style syndicated columnist locked in a sycophantic tango. The aptly named Sidney Falco (Curtis), a bird of prey if there ever was one, sacrifices everything and everyone to further his ambition. His keeper, J. J. Hunsecker (Lancaster), who fully appreciates Falco's pliability, exploits him even as he sadistically humiliates him. *Sweet Smell* is a gritty exposé of the role of the press agent—a job that, in this film, is radically sycophantic. But almost sixty years after its release, *Sweet Smell* seems a prescient comment on our own economy, in which go-betweens and fixers abound in workplaces where the product is an intangible, like "access" or "notice."

Falco's particularly vile brand of sycophancy is established early in the film. We see him evade irate clients who see no benefit from the money they pay him. Falco seeks to blackmail a married columnist who has slept with a cigarette girl, Rita. After arranging to meet Rita later at his apartment, Sidney then pimps her to yet another columnist for a favor. Curtis's acting skill is especially in evidence in this sleazy scene, as he cajoles and menaces Rita into acquiescence. "What am I, a tangerine that peels in a minute?" laments Rita, but, kicking off a shoe and taking a drink, she complies. By turns smarmy, eloquent, and crude, Sidney's cynicism takes many shapes.

Front and center in the film is the relation between sycophant and target. Falco cringes, wheedles, fawns, and comes to Hunsecker's every whistle. It's clear that the columnist relishes the flattery and obedience he commands. "Match me," he curtly orders Falco, barely extending his cigarette as he pauses in a particularly humiliating account of the sleazy world of the press agent to a table of his guests. And Sidney brilliantly responds; his entire body tenses and coils with obsequious attention to his master. Hunsecker's attitude toward his creature combines admiration, disgust, and calculation. Watching Falco at work, and momentarily struck by the sweet-faced charm that Falco can muster, Hunsecker muses: "I'd hate to take a bite out of you. You're a cookie laced with arsenic."

The script emphasizes the fact that even such aggressively cynical characters underestimate the corrosive power of sycophancy. The plot turns on Hunsecker's efforts to break his sister's attachment to Steve, a young jazz musician. By employing the superserviceable Falco, Hunsecker distances himself from his machinations, appearing blameless. Falco arranges a meeting at which he needles Susan's suitor into an attack on Hunsecker's journalistic ethics, which J. J. quickly uses to secure a promise from his sister that she will break off the engagement. So far, so good for this sinister pair. Sidney's skills in manipulation and improvisation are evident as he goads Steve while allowing J. J. to maintain a facade of brotherly concern. Equally apparent is Hunsecker's subtle management of Sidney during the confrontation, his wordless complicity as Falco circles his prey.

Susan's capitulation, however complete, does not satisfy her brother. Stung by Steve's heartfelt denunciation of his phony patriotism, Hunsecker demands that Sidney destroy him. Conniving with a corrupt policeman, J. J. insists that Falco plant marijuana on Steve. Sidney resists this scheme, which he considers excessive, but, like Rita earlier, he gives in. The musician is arrested, beaten savagely, and taken to the hospital. Susan learns of the plot and leaves her brother. Hunsecker, drunk on Sidney's flatteries, overreaches and loses his sister. Sidney, having made himself the willing instrument of his own ambitions, finds that he cannot ultimately shed the role of sycophant. He has become the role he has played so well, and the illusion of control and autonomy with which he comforted himself amid the many humiliations of his relationship with J. J. falls away. Sidney ends in the gutter, beaten by Hunsecker's vicious police stooge, as Susan steps into the morning light.

The movie is a satisfying melodrama in which the evil are punished and the good, if not rewarded, are permitted to escape the corrupt world of J. J. and Sidney. Few movies create such a menace for innocence. Hunsecker's need to possess his sister (a drive so dark that the film can only hint at it with a lurid sequence in which J. J., rigid and menacing, looms over his sister as she sleeps) sparks the action, but Falco's sycophancy acts as an accelerant. The movie takes the suck-up's viewpoint: this is the story of Sidney's ambitions, energy, cleverness, and downfall. Whatever the satisfactions of seeing evil punished and virtue set free, *Sweet Smell of Success* also provides close scrutiny of sycophancy. The movie brilliantly explores the subtle codependency of flatterer and target, their intricate dance of service and sadism, and the failure of both parties to understand how little control they have over their relationship. Both Falco and Hunsecker smugly assume they are in charge of the situation, that they each play a role they can step in and out of as its suits them. Neither can.

Film, as opposed to other media, magnifies one aspect of sycophancy. No one who watches Curtis in *Sweet Smell of Success*—his lightning shifts among roles as he plays off and manipulates those around him—can help but think about sycophancy as a performance. Curtis's Falco is a trickster, and while we do not approve of him, we certainly note his facility and ingenuity. Watching an

Screenshot from *Sweet Smell of Success:* Sidney Falco
(Tony Curtis) lighting J. J. Hunsecker's (Burt Lancaster) cigarette.

actor in a role that is defined by acting and role-playing gives the film unexpected depth, especially as it uses this intensely self-referential presentation to explore the connections between sycophancy and acting.

Finally, *Sweet Smell of Success* anticipates a salient feature of the modern workplace. In 1957, the script needed to explain the shapeless occupation of press agent—a job without a tangible product, set hours, or a determinate workplace—to the audience. The essentials of the job—access and influence—are far more familiar to many workers today, as is its essentially contingent nature. If one must, like Sidney, please to live, then one must live to please, and sycophancy seems the inevitable means to this questionable end.

Smithers: Sunny-Side Up Sycophancy

The small screen offers its own particular take on sycophancy. No one expects three-dimensionality from a cartoon. But the severe reduction of such a medium provides a close look at the elements of the sycophantic exchange—a kind of X-ray that probes beneath the skin of ingratiation. *The Simpsons*, surely one of the greatest cartoons of all time, provides an exemplary flatterer in the character of Smithers. Anticipating every need of Mr. Burns's, his robber-baron boss, catering to his every whim, and ignoring all insults, Smithers is the always-obliging "let me do that for you, sir" yes-man. If one must, as Sydney Falco's ambiguous position implies, live to please in the undefined space of the modern workplace, Smithers is the reductio ad absurdum of corporate sycophancy.

The force of this characterization lies in its simplicity and repetition. *The Simpsons* doesn't say anything new or surprising about sycophancy or the effects of sycophancy in the workplace. Smithers swoons over everything Mr. Burns does, even as his boss belittles him mercilessly. Like anything that's repeated, the challenge for the show's creators is to vary his sycophancy enough to make it funny each time. However, the serial form of the program gives this representation a kind of satiric force that makes us laugh even as we recognize a basic truth of many contemporary work situations.

The episode from the second season, "Burns Verkaufen der Kraftwerk," in which Mr. Burns sells his nuclear power plant to a German corporation, shows the comic extremes of Smithers's sycophancy. The show begins with a buoyant Smithers washing Mr. Burns's nearly bald head with baby shampoo, bubbling as he energetically lathers: "It's formulated to rinse clean with no oily deposits. And mild enough to use daily. Isn't life grand? What's wrong, sir? Did I get some in your eyes? The shampoo specifically said, 'No more tears.'" Part of the humor here lies in the precise association of advertising language with Smithers's abasement. Advertising—quintessentially sycophantic—becomes the script for this most cheerful of flatterers. The sycophant uses the blandishments of selling as a soundtrack for his own degradation.

Despite Smithers's tap-dancing sycophancy, Mr. Burns is depressed. Running the power plant has lost its appeal. Even Smithers's attempts to cheer him up by bringing out a sock puppet of

Snappy the Alligator provide no relief. Smithers is so attached to Mr. Burns he can't help seeing everything through the lens of his boss. In the next scene Smithers sees Homer kicking the candy dispenser after it eats his dollar. Mistaking the cause of Homer's hissy fit, Smithers thinks Homer is glum because of Mr. Burns's unhappiness. Here the focus of the sycophant—the doggy-looking-at-a-doorknob intensity of his involvement with the target—bends every aspect of reality to the sycophantic function. There is no outside perspective for Smithers.

Having decided to sell the nuclear plant, Mr. Burns discusses the transaction with two German businessmen in a bar. Hearing his boss speak German, Smithers gushes in admiration as Mr. Burns informs the men, "Mein Kriecher sagte mir, dass ich nie aufhoere, ihn zu erstaunen" (My lickspittle told me that I never cease to amaze him). In the next scene we see Smithers studying Sycophantic German and repeating phrases like "You looken sharpen todayen, mein herr," and "that was a gutsy decision, sir." Seeing Mr. Burns tending to his bees after selling the plant, Smithers blithely endures multiple bee stings as he chats with his former boss. No gesture of devotion is beyond him.

However exaggerated this picture of sycophancy in the workplace might seem, one need only glance at recent events for an uncanny confirmation. Our current president, unhappy with the official tally of votes he garnered in the election as well as the relatively small crowds that attended his inauguration, dispatched numerous operatives to offer what one spokesperson has since called "alternative facts." No evidence went unchallenged, and no possible scenario, however far-fetched, was unexplored as various administration flunkys rushed to soothe their boss's injured feelings with accusations of massive voter fraud and concerted media bias. And these sycophants, sadly, lack the amiable charm of Smithers.

One can only marvel at the show's series of witty variations on Smithers's chirpy toadying—whether he's festooned head to toe in Mr. Burns's campaign buttons when his boss runs for governor ("Two Cars in Every Garage and Three Eyes on Every Fish"), pedaling furiously on a bike to exercise Mr. Burns as his boss

sits complacently ("Who Shot Mr. Burns, pt. 1"), happily turning on a fire hose so Mr. Burns can spray striking workers ("Last
Exit to Springfield"), or complimenting the way his boss abuses
others. Smithers cheerfully endures insults even when his boss
comments on the "shocking decline in his toadying" as Smithers
ventures to advise Mr. Burns not to take over Springfield's local
school when oil is found on its grounds ("Who Shot Mr. Burns,
pt. 1").

    The character of Smithers was apparently inspired by the bow-
ing and scraping of Fox executives around Barry Diller when he
headed the network. Matt Groening, the creator of *The Simpsons*,
and his collaborators have distilled the essence of fawning in
Smithers, whose sycophancy testifies to the durability of the stereotype and ubiquity of the behavior. In the cartoon workplace,
employees are reduced to stock types: on *The Simpsons*, we have
Homer the slacker and Smithers the sycophant. The ingenuity of
the show's writers lies in their ability to find endless new permu-
tations of Smithers's behavior. This indeed is the charm of the
running joke, which redounds to the writers' skill, not their depth
of analysis. We can ride the train as spectators forever, observers
amused and uneasy by turns. But we also might like to consider
sycophancy in other ways.

Transformative Sycophancy

"We Have Met the Enemy, and He Is Us"

Up to now, we've mostly looked at situations in which sycophants know exactly what they are doing. They choose sycophancy, and they accept their humiliations and abasements as a means to an end. Like those early Greek meddlers, the original *sykophantes*, their actions are calculated. Quid pro unctuous quo.

But literature, time and again, reminds us that life is rarely so tidy. The transactional model of sycophancy explains only so much. In the late nineteenth and early twentieth centuries, as writers began to experiment with technique and expand their subject matter, the older model of sucking up, with its antiquated psychological understanding, seemed narrow. A novel like Marcel Proust's *In Search of Lost Time*, with its obsessive focus on society and manners, class, and social climbing, could not fail to treat sycophancy. Much has been said about the prominence of snobs and snobbery in the book, but we can just as easily see this feature as an indication of the prevalence of sycophancy. Every snob in Proust begins by sucking up.

Two considerations are in order as we approach Proust's masterpiece. First, the novel is known for being long, but it is the complexity of the author's storytelling that makes reading it so demanding. The book, as its title suggests, is a memoir of sorts—a memoir with a doubled time framework. Simply put, the young Marcel reports, and the older Marcel comments and explains. Proust's narration blends the younger Marcel's experience, necessarily limited, with the older Marcel's retrospective understanding. In fact, the meaning of an experience often unfolds long after the moment, through a flash of insight triggered by physical sensation. In addition, the older, wiser Marcel also withholds information. So while his life story is bifurcated—comprising the lived experience, with its immediacy and force and sensory detail, and the memory of it, with its surprising revelations—there is also a plot in which the older writer Marcel (like the historical author, Marcel Proust) anticipates certain events or adds new details to parts of the story he has already told.

Second, Proust's characters are capable of profound change, often to the point of unrecognizability. In many novels, the explanation of such transformations is part of the novel's theme, and the contradictions resolve into a unified self. Proust, however, insists that not one but many selves are present to each character. For example, it comes as a surprise to learn that Marcel, a foppish and convalescent aesthete who drifts through life pursuing sensations, has fought several duels. This revelation, almost an aside, comes long after its chronological place in the story. Clearly Proust intends an abrupt, retrospective change in our attitude toward the younger Marcel. This element of vertiginous surprise is one of the great themes of *In Search of Lost Time*.

Proust structures his novel as if it were a house of mirrors for the protagonist Marcel. Many—perhaps all—of the characters reflect the narrator's own faults and foibles back at him. The characters continue the analysis of the protagonist by isolating or exaggerating the protagonist's features. While this is a familiar device for novelists, Proust's genius lies in his extension of it. More than artistic technique, in Proust it is a reflection of lived human experience. As the narrator observes in *Swann's Way*, "It is only with the passions of others that we are ever really familiar, and what we come to discover about our own can only be learned from them."[1] We learn of ourselves not so much through introspection as through other characters, who either display our own foibles and weaknesses or provide dismaying accounts of our behavior.

Marcel's account of Legrandin, a friend of the family, becomes an anatomy of Marcel as well as a comment on human nature. Legrandin, an engineer who spends his weekends in Combray, Marcel's boyhood home, is well known to the family. Impeccably dressed, articulate, amusing, and artistic, he is for them "the very pattern of a gentleman." Yet the narrator catches Legrandin not once but twice in an ecstasy of sycophancy. First, Marcel and his father encounter Legrandin as they return from church. The latter accompanies a somewhat exclusive local lady known "only by sight" to Marcel's family. They greet their old friend, who, to their bewilderment, barely acknowledges them, and then only "with an air of surprise, as though he had not recognized us" (166). The family later discusses this snub but decides to overlook it. This decision seems justified when, the next evening, Legrandin, strolling alone, hastens to greet the family with outstretched hand, amusing conversation, and particular attention to the progress of Marcel's literary education.

But a few Sundays later, Legrandin cuts the family again, this time even more completely. They watch Legrandin in full sycophantic mode as he is introduced to another exclusive local, the wife of a large landowner. Legrandin toadies shamelessly, bowing "with extraordinary zeal and animation." As Marcel notes, this "obsequious alacrity of the basest sort" produces "a sort of tense muscular wave to ripple over Legrandin's rump" (174). His new idol gives him a menial task to perform—carrying a message to her coachman. "Rapt in a sort of dream" (175) as he carries out his charge, Legrandin pretends not to see Marcel and his family as they pass. His debasement is complete; his absurdity obvious.

Later that same day Marcel and his father meet Legrandin again, once more in the company of the landowner's wife. This time, he deigns to recognize his old friends, but only with a subtle movement of the eyes that he conceals from the lady upon whom he so assiduously attends. These encounters force Marcel to consider "the possibility of a Legrandin altogether different from the one we knew" (175).

Eventually, Marcel brings Legrandin to a crisis with an innocent query—whether he knows the Guermantes, the local nobility that fascinate the narrator and become the object of his own budding sycophancy. The "other" Legrandin, the sycophant/snob, flashes out:

> At the sound of the name Guermantes, I saw in the middle of each of our friend's blue eyes a little brown nick appear, as though they

had been stabbed by some invisible pin-point, while the rest of the pupil reacted by secreting the azure overflow. His fringed eyelids darkened and drooped. His mouth, set in a bitter grimace, was the first to recover, and smiled, while his eyes remained full of pain, like the eyes of a handsome martyr whose body bristles with arrows. (178)

Here are the bitter and inevitable wages of sucking up. Proust brilliantly reenacts Legrandin's mortification. The nicks, stabs, and pricks in the passage give way to a climactic scene of martyrdom, with Legrandin now the St. Sebastian of sycophancy. Pained to admit that the Guermantes do not know him, Legrandin launches into a convoluted series of excuses for his social insignificance. He makes sweeping professions of his independence, his revolutionary or Jacobin sympathies, and his philosophical removal from the world. While the young narrator cannot yet follow all the complexities of Legrandin's sycophancy (and the snobbery that accompanies it), he does understand that the obsequiousness Legrandin adopts toward the upper class requires that he conceal his friendship with middle-class families like Marcel's.

Legrandin's vehement attack on sycophancy is both self-contradictory and sincere. His sycophancy is not, to him, sycophancy, because he has invested the object of his slavish devotion with all the graces and every species of wisdom. Whereas others might view his behavior as fawning and cringing, he does not see it that way himself. Proust is unusually direct in his analysis of Legrandin's blindness: what he calls "the intervening effects of imagination" (181) resolve the contradictions in attitude so apparent to the young Marcel. Wrapped in a mist of the charm that Legrandin himself confers upon her, the landowner's wife becomes his ideal, canceling his sycophancy. In fact, for Legrandin such servility is a testament to his ability to distinguish superior character and development, and thus a marker of taste.

Proust's story of Marcel's confrontation with his own sycophancy is both humorous and indirect. Typically, an incident in Proust takes time to unfold, as many considerations and reconsiderations follow the bare events of the episode. Marcel's lesson in his own sycophancy begins with an offhand remark by a family friend, Norpois, who is a well-placed diplomat. The young Marcel has long been eager to gain access to Madame Swann, her glittering salon, and her daughter. When Norpois offers to convey this admiration to Madame Swann, Marcel can hardly find the means to express his gratitude. He almost kisses Norpois's hands, but he confines his enthusiasm to gushing, "If you would speak to Mme. Swann my whole life would not be long enough to prove my gratitude, and that life would be all at your service."[2] Later Marcel is chagrined to find that Norpois has spoken of his excessive response to the other object of his slavish devotion, the Princess de Guermantes. His fervor has become a joke for Norpois, who terms him, aptly, a "hysterical little flatterer."[3]

Marcel has been following, with some amusement, the obsequiousness of others. Now he has met the enemy in himself and, even more humiliatingly, must confront it through the eyes of others. The mortifications of this anecdote are endless. Not only is he forced to see himself in as demeaning a way as possible, but it is Madame Swann herself, the woman for whom he performed this egregious act of bowing and scraping to Norpois, who informs Marcel of Norpois's ridicule.

This anecdote develops over several volumes. The episode with Norpois occurs early in *Within a Budding Grove*, and it resurfaces, in all its mortifying detail, halfway through the next volume, *The Guermantes Way.* A very discerning reader might note Marcel's own excess in thanking Norpois as it occurs, but clearly Proust wishes readers to experience something of Marcel's surprise when his behavior is revealed to him. As ever, the original moment itself cannot be understood until much later, if at all. Sycophancy is not always a behavior we perform consciously. At the moment, all we know are the "auxiliary motives," the self-flattering purposes and rationalizations that we give our obsequious behaviors.

Marcel's lessons in his own sucking up continue. Later, Gilberte, his former playmate and Swann's daughter, informs him that her parents "can't stand you." This bruising appraisal causes Marcel to write Swann a letter to prove "the purity of my inten-

tions, the goodness of my soul" (286). Gilberte's report to Marcel
—that Swann believes the letter "only goes to prove how right
I was" (287)—provides yet another glimpse at Marcel's unconscious sycophancy. The young man's ire at Swann's response is
later tempered, and he muses that "perhaps it was simply that
Swann knew that nobility is often no more than the inner aspect which our egotistical feelings assume when we have not yet
named and classified them" (287). One's point of view is a mixture of egotism and misunderstanding. The narrator later under-
stands that his flattery of Swann was a "secondary veneration,"
an extension of his primary adoration of Madame Swann. Again,
the sycophant is saved from knowledge of his sycophancy by the
"intervening effects of . . . imagination."

Proust carries us far from the unsubtle sycophancies described
by earlier writers. The villainous fawning of, for instance, Shakespeare's Iago can be put in a simple formulation: "I follow him
[Othello] to serve my turn upon him." In Proust, a new, delusional
sycophancy can be discerned, one that hides its purposes, or perhaps redistributes them. Further, given Proust's insistence on the
careful scrutiny of others for access to the truth of our natures,
sycophancy becomes not simply something others do, but a part
of the human condition. It is less to be condemned than pondered
for what it tells us about the circumstances of our world. Indeed,
it is a clue to the nature of the self.

Murderous Sycophancy

Crime novels, whether high-toned *noir* or more downscale pulp
fiction, turn upon primal emotions. Lust, rage, envy—really,
all the seven deadly sins—drive the characters of such works to
extremes of human experience. The force of this genre derives
from a reductive vision of life, which clears away all other considerations for its protagonists. Any higher motivation—altruism,
compassion, even love—becomes an illusion, as characters act according to inescapable impulses or their own interest, considered
in the narrowest terms. Pulps and *noir* do not tell us much about
the sources of these compulsions; they simply accept them. But

they do provide a detailed account of the means through which their protagonists address them. The *why* is simple and elemental, but the *how* is spectacularly detailed.

This emphasis on externals makes the depictions of sycophancy in *noir* fiction unusually rigorous. Like good scientific experiments, these accounts limit the variables in each character's behavior, simplifying and clarifying it for us. *Noir* and pulp fiction are, of course, more akin to thought experiments than empirical studies, but, like good thought experiments, they remain illuminating even as they await so-called real-world confirmation.

Patricia Highsmith's 1955 novel *The Talented Mr. Ripley* furnishes an exceptional example. Highsmith's protagonist, Tom Ripley, is a sycophant, and the novel traces his progress from slavish adulator, cringing and fawning for tokens of approval, to confident, self-directed criminal. By the end of the book, Ripley has begun to develop, with considerable panache, the talents that the title advertises, but in the first hundred pages, Highsmith provides an inside account of the sycophant's perspective.

As in many of her novels, Highsmith begins *The Talented Mr. Ripley* with a chance meeting that her protagonist exploits. Ripley is twenty-five, living hand to mouth in New York City. He works a small-time tax scam, but he is too timid to cash the checks he gets his marks to write. He's bored, resentful, and entirely marginal. Out of the blue, he gets a chance to change his life. The father of a slight acquaintance offers to pay Ripley's expenses to Italy on the condition that he provide an unusual service. Ripley must persuade his son, Dickie Greenleaf, who has been living abroad—and, to his father's mind, shirking his responsibilities to the family business—to return home. Mr. Greenleaf has mistaken the relation of his son and Tom; they are not friends. But Ripley, drawing on his capacities as sycophant, intuits the father's desires and assumes the role of a confidant.

Ripley's talents of ingratiation are formidable. Like Iago, he is quick to imagine what others want. We see this in the first moments of his conversation with Mr. Greenleaf, as Ripley improvises a memory of the last time he saw Dickie:

"I suppose he'll remember me. We were at a weekend party once out on Long Island. I remember Dickie and I went out and gathered mussels, and everyone had them for breakfast." Tom smiled. "A couple of us got sick, and it wasn't a very good party. But I remember Dickie talking that weekend about going to Europe. He must have left just—"

"I remember!" Mr. Greenleaf said. "That was the last weekend Richard was here. I think he told me about the mussels."[4]

Note the craft here. Tom adopts an insinuating modesty ("I *suppose*"), which he follows with a plausible account of the last meeting, providing a plot, and then dangling a possible connection for his target. Mr. Greenleaf eagerly clutches at the reminiscence of his son, taking up the palpable detail of the mussels, which cinches Ripley's bid for Mr. Greenleaf's favor. This deft little exchange shows Ripley's remarkable talent for ingratiation. Tom has imagined a scene whose vivid details enter into Mr. Greenleaf's thoughts.

Warming to his task, Ripley works another slight memory into a rich picture for his target. He recalls seeing some ship models in Dickie's apartment—again, Tom cleverly uses the scant materials at hand to ingratiate himself; boatbuilding is the Greenleaf family business—and this bait draws yet another catch from Mr. Greenleaf's fond memory:

"Those were only childhood efforts!" Mr. Greenleaf was beaming. "Did he ever show you his frame models? Or his drawings?"

Dickie hadn't, but Tom said brightly, "Yes! Of course he did. Pen-and-ink drawings. Fascinating, some of them." Tom had never seen them, but he could see them now, precise draughtsman's drawings with every line and bolt and screw labeled, could see Dickie smiling, holding them up for him to look at, and he could have gone on for several minutes describing details for Mr. Greenleaf's delight, but he checked himself. (8)

This passage brilliantly displays the range and complexity of Tom's sycophancy. His first response is emotional, his "bright" response to Mr. Greenleaf's "beaming" nostalgia. He mirrors and thereby heightens the target's gush of feeling. He proceeds to translate Mr. Greenleaf's words into vivid images. He sees Dickie's drawings, wonderfully elaborated, and conjures up a scene between Dickie and himself. Like Iago, Ripley adopts the target's perspective as if from the inside. He *sees* Mr. Greenleaf's memory, and, by doing so, he is able to further insinuate himself.

Ripley's empathy is so richly imaginative as to constitute a creative act in itself. He wants Mr. Greenleaf's approval, and he forges a series of small but telling emotional connections with him—mostly by seizing on the slightest hint upon which to establish a link between himself and the target. But he progresses rapidly, acting boldly and decisively upon his intuitions. When he meets Dickie in Italy, he resolves to "make Dickie like him" (53), and, when the acquaintance seems to flag, Tom shrewdly recognizes that he must take a risk "to amuse Dickie or to repel him" (56). He resorts to honesty, confessing that he's been sent by Mr. Greenleaf to reclaim him. Ripley's gamble works. Dickie is interested and amused, and Ripley then consolidates his gain by doing amusing impressions, returning to the usual quid pro quo brand of cajoling flattery. But Highsmith makes it clear that Ripley's sycophancy, however calculated, is not entirely rational. There is an excessive and less fully conscious side to Tom's behavior. His mimicry and empathy are not simply techniques he deploys; they are second nature to him. Ripley dedicates himself to meticulous repetition of Dickie's gestures, "adopting his gait" (73), and he imagines a finer nature for Dickie than he possesses. When Dickie shows Tom his paintings, Tom is sorry to see immediately that they are second-rate, "because he wanted Dickie to be much more" (73).

Flatterers often emulate the target; Plutarch ridicules just this kind of behavior in his essay. But Highsmith goes beyond simple mirroring. Ripley creates, through mimicry, the Dickie that he would like to be. When Dickie's girlfriend, Marge, tries to drive a wedge between Tom and his new friend by suggesting that Tom is "queer," Ripley's first reaction is simple anger. First he imagines

Dickie and Marge "embracing" or "touching" (77), then, spying on the couple, he sees them kissing. Returning to Dickie's villa, Tom rampages about his idol's studio, throwing things, like a jealous lover. But Highsmith traces this tangle of sycophancy, sexual jealousy, and rage to more surprising, more primal needs. Ripley's sexuality is, of course, in question here. But his next move shows how reductive it would be to consider this simply a version of the usual *noir* love triangle. Ripley puts on one of Dickie's suits, arranges his hair to be more like his friend's, and, as he looks in the mirror, mimics Dickie's voice: "Marge, you must understand that I don't love you" (78). Entering more fully into the role, Tom then acts out a small, imagined scene between Dickie and Marge, in which, as she tries to hold her lover, he turns violent:

> "Marge, stop it!" Tom turned suddenly and made a grab in the air as if he were seizing Marge's throat. He shook her, twisted her, while she sank lower and lower, until at last he left her, limp, on the floor. He was panting. He wiped his forehead the way Dickie did, reached for a handkerchief and, not finding any, got one from Dickie's top drawer, then resumed in front of the mirror. Even his parted lips looked like Dickie's lips when he was out of breath from swimming, drawn down a little from his lower teeth. "You know why I had to do that," he said, still breathlessly, addressing Marge, although he watched himself in the mirror. "You were interfering between Tom and me—No, not that! But there *is* a bond between us!" (78–79)

The usual reading might invoke the tired notion of "repressed homosexuality" so widely held in the 1950s and 1960s, as Tom at once acts out his desire for Dickie and consciously denies it. But more important to Highsmith is the power that Ripley gains through the emulation of another. He is on one level imagining what he'd like his idol to do, to repudiate Marge. But he also becomes his idol. This sycophancy is ultimately empowering, a sycophancy capable not only of internalizing the target but also of transforming it. The *quo* of the familiar toady-target relation becomes identity with the target. By emulating Dickie, Ripley escapes from a self he despises. He seeks ultimately to replace himself, to become Dickie. All his feelings of dissatisfaction are resolved by the freedom and power of being someone else: "It was impossible," notes Tom later in the novel as he travels to Paris on his victim's money, and in his victim's clothes, "to be lonely or bored . . . so long as he was Dickie Greenleaf" (122).

The plot of *The Talented Mr. Ripley*, in which Tom kills and then impersonates Dickie, has its roots in pulp fiction, but Highsmith entwines this genre with another. There is considerable irony in her choice: she takes up a sturdy nineteenth-century favorite, the bildungsroman, or the novel of development. Ripley's extreme sycophancy, situated within the pulp plot, appears as a personality disorder. In the pattern set by the novel of development, it appears as an enabling stage in Ripley's growth from marginal, self-doubting loser to confident, and even artistic, criminal. The adulatory mimicry in which Ripley reflexively engages—copying Dickie's gait and voice, adopting his tastes—allows him to discover and develop his talents. Through forgery, Tom ultimately forges his own character. His happiness is evident as he exults in his eventual transformation:

> This was the clean slate he had thought about on the boat coming over from America. This was the real annihilation of his past and of himself, Tom Ripley, who was made up of that past, and his rebirth as a completely new person. (127)

Highsmith's cynical humor is evident here, as she provides an ironic version of a familiar American myth. Many writers had explored the figure of the self-made man of the New World; here Highsmith provides a cynical but provocative retelling of this essentially American story.

> Hadn't he learned something from these last months? If you wanted to be cheerful, or melancholic, or wistful, or thoughtful, or courteous, you simply had to *act* those things with every gesture. (193)

As Ripley sheds his sycophancy, he becomes more and more pragmatic. It isn't thinking that makes things so, nor is it knowing oneself that is important. It's all a question of choice, resolve, and action. You are what you do, says Highsmith's protagonist, and the emulation of sycophancy allows one to understand this.

As the risky plots Tom has brilliantly improvised draw to a crisis, he sums up his progress with brio. Surrounded by dangers, but exhilarated by them, he imagines a voyage to Greece:

> He would see the islands, swimming for the first time into his view, as a living, breathing, courageous individual—not as some cringing little nobody from Boston. (277)

Ripley's transformation is complete, as he hails the emergence of his new self—the dynamic and decisive criminal he has become. He conjures up a barrage of classical references as he imagines his approach to Greece, "standing in the wind at the prow of a ship, crossing the wine-dark sea like Jason or Ulysses returning" (277). Highsmith finds unexpected value in sycophancy—in the intensification of artistic sensibility and in the production of an autonomous self.

Noir fiction offers its readers the exhilaration of vicarious danger and the allure of the forbidden. It challenges the audience's everyday views of human nature, revealing a brutal world of compulsion and necessity. Highsmith's novel revels not only in Tom's criminality—his newfound freedom of action—but also in the subversion of other values. Sycophancy becomes the path to self-transformation. Tom begins as one of Plutarch's weak sycophants, aping the target's superficial traits, dancing attendance, and making himself small. He then imagines himself as the target—or more precisely, as a better version of his idol. Tom becomes Dickie, but he is also more than Dickie, and the facility he develops by imitation becomes a means of radical change. For Ripley, the way up is the way down. Through sycophancy and imitation, he cuts the ties to his old "cringing" self to become the Jason or Ulysses of his dreams.

How Low Can One Go?

So far we've traced a paradox in the way we think about sycophancy. It's clear that intention matters in recognizing this behavior. The same act can be ingratiating or benign, depending upon the motivation behind it. Presumably, once we've established these intentions, we can distinguish, as Plutarch puts it, "a flatterer from a friend." But, as Edward E. Jones laments, intentions are "cognitively inaccessible," not only to those on the receiving end of sycophancy or those watching it transpire between others but sometimes to the sycophant as well. This ambiguity stymies the scientist, who must rely on subjects whose self-reporting and judgment of others is suspect. But to the novelist, who has developed powerful tools to explore the uncertainties of human behavior, such dubious territory is familiar. The novelist need not resolve the ambiguities of the situation; he reports them, in all their indeterminate and contradictory detail. By describing them, he calls upon readers to consider these uncertainties in the light of their own experience.

Even modern commercial fiction can provide a visceral sense of the self-loathing that sycophants feel as they ply their slimy trade. Andrea, the protagonist of Lauren Weisberger's *The Devil Wears Prada*, unfailingly registers her self-disgust even as she performs on cue. When castigated by her endlessly abusive boss, Miranda Priestly, for being unavailable—or more exactly, being on a flight that had been delayed and having to go through customs like every traveler—she apologizes immediately: "I could feel my face grow hot with humiliation. Humiliation at being spoken to that way, but, more than anything, my own shame in pandering to it."[1] Only the prospect of reward for sycophancies rendered makes this tolerable. Asked by her boss whether her experience on the job—largely being a flunky who fetches coffee, runs er-

rands, and placates her boss's bratty children—has been beneficial, she leaps immediately to DEFCON 1 levels of brownnosing:

> "Oh, of course," I gushed. "I've learned more in one year work-
> ing for you than I could've hoped to have learned in any other job.
> It's been fascinating, really, seeing how a major—the major—
> magazine runs, the production cycle, what all the different jobs
> are. And, of course, being able to observe the way you manage
> everything, all the decisions you make—it's been an amazing
> year. I'm so thankful, Miranda!" (326)

Andrea again justifies this hyperbolic bit of fraudulence by
thinking at once of the advantages she will gain from such self-
abasement. In fact, her first concern is whether her raptures
might be too excessive to be effective: "Could this possibly sound
believable? I stole a glance, and she seemed to be buying it, nod-
ding her head gravely" (326).

Although the situation in *The Devil Wears Prada* is comically exaggerated, we are nevertheless comfortably within the workplace
realm imagined by recent IM research. Miranda might demean
Andrea, even to the point of hot tears, but Andrea persists in the
instrumental exchange of her absolute loyalty for benefits to follow. Like Iago, who serves "only to serve my turn upon him"—that
is, he follows his own interest in following—Andrea preserves the
illusion of her toadying as a rational transaction that she controls.
More revealing are Andrea's occasional moments of uncertainty
about her motives. As she rationalizes yet another imposition on
her boyfriend, lobbing excuse after shabby excuse in defense of
her neglect, Andrea realizes that

> all things non-Miranda somehow ceased to be relevant the mo-
> ment I arrived at work. In some ways I still didn't understand
> and certainly couldn't explain—never mind ask anyone else to
> understand—how the outside world just melted into nonexis-
> tence, that the only thing remaining when everything else van-
> ished was *Runway* [the magazine she works for]. It was especially
> difficult to explain this phenomenon when it was the single thing

in my life I despised. And yet, it was the only one that mattered. (222)

How low can one go? Apparently even to these depths, at which the sycophant simply cancels the self in the pursuit of maximum obsequiousness. And apparently one can inhabit this strange space without making any real efforts to explain oneself. Andrea does not seek to justify her behavior by insisting on the importance of the magazine or the eminence of her boss. It remains a mystery.

Yet it is the kind of mystery that cannot stand. We want to know why sycophants pursue such merciless campaigns of self-nullification. One might note that the movie *The Devil Wears Prada* adds scenes that make much of *Runway*'s cultural and artistic impact as well as Miranda's dedication to her job as a calling. Andrea's coworker Nigel gives a heartfelt account of how *Runway* rescued him as a lonely teenager in Rhode Island, and Miranda herself, in perhaps the only exchange with Andrea that seems frank and personal, notes how bitterly she resents the intrusion of her private failures upon the reputation of the magazine. But then the movie is a much better version of events all around than the novel. The film seems to sense the inadequacy of Weisberger's original scenario.

It must be said that readers accept the description of Andrea's emptiness as a real phenomenon, even if it remains a puzzle. Other novels, however, do far more than simply register such states of mind. Kazuo Ishiguro's *The Remains of the Day* scrutinizes the strange psychology of sycophancy. Ishiguro's protagonist, Stevens, who also serves as narrator, is an aging English butler, one used to grand service in Darlington, an aristocratic home, but now heading a reduced staff for a new American owner. Over the course of the novel, as Stevens drives west to meet the former housekeeper at Darlington (whom he consistently misaddresses by her maiden name as Miss Kenton), he ponders his life of devoted service to Lord Darlington. His reminiscences reveal that Darlington had been a Nazi sympathizer and apologist before the war, for which he spent the remainder of his life in disgrace.

Stevens's anxiety about the nature of service is acute. Much of his narration is defensive, a kind of anxious special pleading that seeks to justify the pandering and humiliation that his job requires. He carefully develops his professional ethos throughout the novel through a series of anecdotes, from which he draws certain maxims illustrative of a good or even "great" butler. These ideas center on the butler's ability to maintain his "dignity," whether in the face of unusual challenges to household order, such as the presence of a tiger in an Indian nabob's dining room, or the petty humiliations and insults endured from the master or his guests. A "great" butler will, according to Stevens, only "abandon the professional being he inhabits" when he pleases.[2]

This ethos serves Stevens well in several demeaning encounters. For instance, when a guest, seeking to demonstrate to the other gentlemen the limitations of democracy, quizzes Stevens with questions about trade relations, the national debt, the relation of currency issues to pending arms agreements, or North African policy, Stevens is able to perform satisfactorily:

> [I] saw the situation for what it was; that is to say, it was clearly expected that I be baffled by the question. Indeed, in the moment or so that it took for me to perceive this and compose a suitable response, I may even have given the outward impression of struggling with the question, for I saw all the gentlemen in the room exchange mirthful smiles. (195)

So long as Stevens can "inhabit" the role, he can make himself small for the amusement of the guests without any sense of ignominy. He convinces himself that he keeps his reputation and dignity so long as he performs well. When the questioner satisfies himself as to the ignorance and incompetence of "our good man here" as well as that of "the few million others like him" (196), the room erupts with "open, hearty laughter" at Stevens's expense. Despite the aggression in this humiliation, in which class plays an ugly part, Stevens consoles himself by recalling that "any decent professional should expect to take such events in his stride" (196).

Key for Stevens's maintenance of dignity here is the illusion of choice. He controls his deference, and he plays along with the role, even heightening the comedy by appearing to flounder as he is questioned. Stevens makes himself small out of profession-alism. A "great" butler, according to Stevens, is one who "has ap-plied his talents to serving a great gentleman—and through the latter, to serving humanity" (117). With this bit of legerdemain, Stevens transforms a range of sycophantic roles—from the "yes-man" to the reliable doormat—into something positive, even a kind of humanitarian benevolence.

Yet this larger sense of service cannot relieve Stevens's anx-iety. He is alive to certain disruptions of this scenario—small, dimly recalled episodes that call his adulation of Darlington into question. Twice he denies having served Lord Darlington, and he realizes that he should "account for such distinctly odd behavior" (122) to his readers. Stevens struggles with these denials, which imply shame at an association to which he devoted his life, and he concludes his meditations on his behavior with a remarkable profession of allegiance:

> You will appreciate that to have served his lordship at Darling-ton Hall during those years was to come as close to the hub of this world's wheel as one such as I could ever have dreamt. I gave thirty-five years' service to Lord Darlington; one would surely not be unjustified in claiming that during those years, one was, in the truest terms, "attached to a distinguished household." In looking back over my career thus far, my chief satisfaction derives from what I achieved during those years, and I am today nothing but proud and grateful to have been given such a privilege. (126)

Stevens's rhetoric—delivered with all the pomposity and false modesty of a public speech—is the perfect form for this soaring but blinkered devotion. That such a job, whatever one's sense of professional responsibilities, would be a "privilege" that prompts pride and gratitude does more than strain credulity. It reveals the flaw in Stevens's justification of his professional life, the danger that one's "duty" might collapse into mere sycophancy.

Ishiguro might have plotted the novel more conventionally, allowing Stevens to recall his evasions, understand them as symp-toms, and repudiate his illusions about his employer. Stevens might, in whatever day remains to him, confront what his situation and the social forces of midcentury Britain have done to him. But the brilliance of this novel lies in Ishiguro's maintenance of his narrator's unreliability. Stevens is always on the verge of unhappy revelations about himself, Lord Darlington, and the nature of his service. Like a word forever on the tip of one's tongue, this full consciousness never emerges.

With Stevens's extermination of self, we seem to have reached the limits of sycophantic self-nullification. How could one suppress so completely the simple claims of self—to judge, to maintain one's basic dignity, even to feel? But the thought experiments of fiction push further and further into this void at the heart of sycophancy. Most people recall Salman Rushdie's 1988 novel *The Satanic Verses* less as literary fiction than as an event. Few people have read the book; its fame rests on the *fatwa* issued against the author by the Ayatollah Khomeini, who deemed the book blasphemous and encouraged Rushdie's murder. But the novel's themes of cultural mixing and transformation through migration are surprisingly connected to the question of sycophancy's power to obliterate the self.

The novel follows a pair of Indian actors, Saladin Chamcha and Gibreel Farishta, who, when their hijacked plane is blown apart over the English Channel, fall to earth miraculously intact. During this plunge to the ground, "embracing head to tail," they pass through a bizarre medium:

> Pushing their way out of the white came a succession of cloud-forms, ceaselessly metamorphosing, gods into bulls, women into spiders, men into wolves. Hybrid cloud-creatures pressed in upon them, gigantic flowers with human breasts dangling from fleshy stalks, winged cats, centaurs, and Chamcha in his semi-consciousness was seized by the notion that he, too, had acquired the quality of cloudiness, becoming metamorphic, hybrid, as if he were growing into the person whose head nestled now between his legs and whose legs were wrapped around his long, patrician neck.[3]

This fantastic downward flight, with its ceaseless transformation, epitomizes Rushdie's theme. Modernity, with its transnational flows of people, capital, and cultural traditions, has rendered time-honored concepts, such as the authentic or stable self, irrelevant. Rushdie provides his protagonists with suitable backstories to support this theme. Gibreel Farishta's rise from humble fast-food delivery boy to Bollywood star has been made possible by his ability to play all the gods of the Hindu pantheon in a series of theological films, from elephant-headed Ganesh (in a mask) to Hanuman the monkey king (in a tail). Chamcha, who has emigrated to Britain, has built a career on his uncanny mimicry, his ability to ventriloquize any male voice necessary for radio or animation. Each masters, effortlessly, whatever role he is given.

Rushdie directly connects sycophancy with this thematic material. Chamcha has adopted a studied British manner—becoming the stereotype of the perfect English gentleman. His name, once Chamchawala but shortened for professional reasons, has a residual meaning when he returns to India, as the locals teasingly point out. "Chamcha" is both "spoon" and "sycophant." As an old friend puts it, "You name yourself Mister Toady and you expect us not to laugh" (55). Chamcha's Anglification is inextricably bound up with questions of sycophancy.

Despite the immediacy of the connection, Rushdie leaves it to the reader to work out the details of the link he posits between transformation and sycophancy. Chamcha's sycophancy has no particular target—his desire is to be more British than the British. As his father puts it bitterly, "He has made himself into an imitator of non-existing men" (72). By abstracting flattery from the immediate exchange between two people, Rushdie prompts us to consider this behavior from another angle, less as a means of exchange adopted by the toady—a *quid* for a desired *quo*—than as a kind of end in itself. Sycophancy is a flight from one's own character and history.

Rushdie's study of sycophancy is not deep. There are none of the nuances about flattery that we see in Proust or in Shakespeare. But his stroke is bold. He frames a certain kind of cultural interaction in terms of sycophancy. Chamcha's evacuation of self, his seamless assimilation of so-called Britishness, is one response to the pressure of global culture. By contrast, his coprotagonist (whose name, Farishta, double-designates him as angelic) stands for the other extreme of transformation. Gibreel masters the art of superficial change, donning and doffing roles and costumes as the job requires. In life he is always himself, despite his facility in embodying what his audience desires.

Chamcha's story explores—in Rushdie's characteristically far-fetched plot—the norms of Britishness. After his fall from the sky, he is picked up, without documentation, by the immigration police. Before, Chamcha's compliance was simply an act of bad faith. Now it becomes a horrifying loss of control. Sycophancy ultimately cedes all authority to the other. Rushdie makes this point extravagantly, by having Chamcha physically change, first sprouting horns, then goat-like hoofs, then losing his precious voice in guttural cries and grunts. Chamcha enters a nightmarish world in which he becomes the animal that the brutal and racist immigration officers describe him as. After a lifetime spent following the norms of Britishness, he is forced to assume the shape of British racial stereotypes and prejudices.

For all its playful, postmodern excess, Rushdie's novel recommends a traditional middle way between extremes. The empty self of the toady and the invulnerable, unchanging authenticity of Gibreel are both inadequate. Rushdie leaves it to one of his most sympathetic characters, Zeenat Viral, to articulate the middle path. Zeeny, a "rash, bad girl" (52) whom Chamcha knew before emigrating to London, has retained all of her outlaw spirit. She barges into his dressing room and immediately puts Chamcha's cultural sycophancy under scrutiny: "Listen, can you escape from all these palefaces and come with us wogs? Maybe you forgot what that is like" (52). At once doctor, homeless advocate, social activist, and author, Zeeny embodies hybridity and openness to change. Her writing makes this clear. She attacks what she terms "the confining myth of authenticity" to recommend "an ethic of historically validated eclecticism" (52). Indian culture— and clearly, for Rushdie, every culture—is "based on the principle of borrowing whatever clothes seemed to fit, Aryan, Mughal, British, take-the-best-and-leave-the-rest" (52). Zeeny's ethic slips between the extremes of pliant sycophancy and everlasting fundamentalism, Chamcha's empty self and Gibreel's impenetrable ego.

How low can one go in sycophancy? Ishiguro and Rushdie remind us of the power of fiction to chart these depths. Stevens's evasions are not fully explicable, but, because of Plutarch's "flatterer within," we recognize them. Stevens's case doesn't so much inform us as remind us that the sycophant's viewpoint, his full absorption into the role, his insistence on rules and abstract notions of duty, dignity, and future advantage, create a formidable bulwark against full consciousness of his obsequious behavior. Rushdie takes a more fantastic route, through a magical tale, but he too turns us back to everyday life and its familiar conventions. The notion that one can deploy sycophancy at will, slipping fluidly in and out of the role without consequences, is a dangerous fallacy. Habit is a great master, and habits of obsequiousness, over time, harden into one's character. And while the ingenuity of the sycophant's plots against others might seem formidable, it pales by comparison to the sycophant's cunning self-deceptions.

What to Do?

What, then, to do? Let's examine some of the options. First, there is the dream of resistance. For the most fantastic version of this response—the nuclear option to sycophancy—we might consider the reply of the Zaporozhian Cossacks of the Ukraine to the Turkish sultan Mohammed IV. The event, if true, took place in 1676 after the Cossacks had repulsed the Ottoman forces. Despite the defeat, the sultan demanded in an imperious letter that the Cossacks submit to Turkish rule:

> An Ultimatum from the Turkish Sultan Mohammed IV to the Zaporozhian Cossacks
>
> I, the Sultan, son of Mahomet, brother of the son and moon, grandson and envoy of God, ruler of all the tsardoms: Macedonia, Babylon, Jerusalem, Great and Small Egypt, the unconquerable, the relentless preserver of the grave of Jesus Christ, the trustee

of God Himself, the hope and strength of the Moslems, the con-
founder and great defender of the Christians, command you, the
Zaporozhian Cossacks—to surrender yourselves to me voluntar-
ily without any struggle and not disturb me with your attacks.

The reply drafted by Ivan Sirko and his comrades is a masterpiece
of insolence:

The Zaporozhian Cossacks' Answer to the Turkish Sultan Mohammed IV

You, Sultan, the Turkish Shaitan [Satan] and the brother and
comrade of the damned devil, of the secretary of Lucifer himself.

You, the knight of the devil, will bare your ass and kill no one.

The devil will hoist you out and you and your troops will be
devoured.

You are a son of a bitch unfit for the pigs of Christians. We are
not afraid of your troops: on land and sea we will beat them and
you, hostile son of the devil and mother fucker.

You are a Jerusalem tinker, a Macedonian wheelwright, a
Babylonian cook, and Alexandrian goat slaughterer, an Arme-
nian pig, a Tartar hangman of goats, a Kamenetsky cat butcher, a
Podolsky scoundrel, a tender of pigs of Great and Small Egypt, a
Lutheran childbirth pain, a swindler of all the world and snake of
the underworld, grandson of the asp itself, a noodle of our God,
a pig's snout, a mare's ass, a dog slaughterer, a pagan forehead,
go to Hell.

From this you know the answer of the Cossacks to your despi-
cableness, now we finish. We don't know dates or possess a calen-
dar, just the moon in the heavens, but there will come such a day
when you will kiss our asses.

Ivan Sirko for the entire clan of Zaporozhians.[4]

Not much conformity of opinion here, however well-managed
the impression. Every pompous claim of the sultan's is met with
a vulgar reversal. The reply is as direct as the circumstances are
elemental: If the Turks want to howl on the edges of the barren
steppes like wolves, they're welcome to it.

Part of the attraction here lies in the insolence and wit of the reply, but another part lies in its remoteness. In the mundane world of organizational charts, we are encouraged, even obliged to respond in more measured terms—to contain rather than rebel against sycophancy. Machiavelli provides a pragmatic response to the problem in his treatise on statecraft, *The Prince*. His treatment is short but pithy. Machiavelli defines a flatterer in the broadest terms, as someone always "thinking more of his own interests . . . and seeking inwardly his own profit in everything."[5] Courts are full of flatterers, and princes are vulnerable because they are often "self-complacent in their affairs" (191). On the other hand, precautions against flattery have consequences. "There is no other way of guarding oneself from flatterers except letting men understand that to tell you the truth does not offend you," Machiavelli observes, "but when every one may tell you the truth, respect for you abates" (191). The cure in this case, allowing everyone to speak the truth as they see it, enfeebles the patient. One can either do nothing and be duped by sycophantic courtiers, or one can act and lose authority.

Machiavelli proposes a compromise. He advises his prince to allow carefully chosen councilors to speak their minds, but only when asked. He should listen carefully, but the prince should make his own decisions. Once a course of action has been taken, other advice should be disregarded, and the prince should follow his decision resolutely.

Like much of Machiavelli's advice, this recommendation is more practical than morally or philosophically satisfying. He simplifies the world's complexities by reduction and exclusion, which allows for action. He does not address the nature of flattery or the flatterer, nor does he concern himself with the difficulties of distinguishing it from other behavior. He treats sycophancy as a given, and he seeks to find ways of protecting his prince from its consequences. Machiavelli considers only what he observes—outward behaviors and results.

Perhaps it is no surprise that Machiavelli's precepts for managing flatterers recall the "best practices" that recent management theory has fetishized. Machiavelli cares little for the moral questions that Plutarch makes central to his philosophy. The world being imperfect, he is willing to act without definite knowledge. The prince needn't concern himself with justice or truth, only with the maintenance of his position. Machiavelli accepts error and ignorance in taking the precautions he advises. For him, behavior matters more than intention, and, insofar as behavior is ambiguous, even behavior doesn't matter much. One acts according to one's axioms; one does not assess particular behaviors and respond to them.

Sycophancy, for some, is the human equivalent of chimps grooming one another—a kind of binding social ritual in which one, as the saying goes, "goes along to get along." Perhaps the most eloquent proponent of this strategy is Philip Dormer Stanhope, the Earl of Chesterfield, who in *Letters to His Son* frankly counsels the cultivation of flattery as an art.[6] "Intrinsic merit will not do," he opines; "services done, or offered" and "expressions of regard and esteem" (March 9, 1748) are necessary for success. One must, in conversation, "take the hue" of anyone one wishes "to be upon terms with" (February 28, 1751). Chesterfield carries his cynicism more easily does than Machiavelli, but he has no higher opinion of human nature:

> If a man has a mind to be thought wiser, and a woman handsomer than they really are, their error is a comfortable one to themselves, and an innocent one with regard to other people; and I would rather make them my friends, by indulging them in it, than my enemies, by endeavoring (and that to no purpose) to undeceive them. (October 16, 1747)

We are far from the flinty brand of friendship imagined by Plutarch. Chesterfield advises his son to be a kind of chameleon, carefully tuning his response to the target's weaknesses, relying on manners and polish to conceal his deceit. In defending his advice Chesterfield goes pretty far:

> That happy talent, the art of pleasing, which so few do, though almost all might possess, is worth all your learning and knowledge

put together. The latter can never raise you high without the former; but the former may carry you, as it has carried thousands, a great way without the latter. (May 23, 1751)

This is an easygoing but boundless cynicism that, pushed far enough, could countenance just about any deception. Rarely does Chesterfield set any limits to flattery. All his concern is for its judicious application. *Suaviter in modo, fortiter in re*, Chesterfield recommends again and again to his young son: "Gentle in manner, resolutely in action." But the *re* here, the action itself—or, more precisely, the knowledge, learning, or morality of the case—counts for little. How a thing is done is everything. Sycophancy, for Chesterfield, carries the day.

Resistance, containment, or submission all seem inadequate—each a combination of wishful thinking, futility, humiliation, credulity, and misjudgment of the problem. One might argue that the entire question of sycophancy relies on a particular kind of social and economic order, durable hierarchies that feature face-to-face negotiation between rulers and the ruled, higher and lower classes, or layers of bureaucracy. Aristocratic privilege and courts breed sycophants—even to the point of ritualizing abasement as bowing and kneeling become prescribed behavior. Despots inspire loyal armies of toadies. The rise of capitalism might seem to offer some escape from enforced sycophancy in the freedom of rational individuals to trade and contract based upon their own interests. But the company man quickly developed a repertoire of ingratiating tactics, as the IM literature lavishly documents. The recent reconfiguration of the workplace—the aggressive delayering of companies, the so-called "flat" world of global commerce—again seems to offer some respite. After all, a workplace premised on the casualization of labor, in which work is performed by contract and often without the intensive face-to-face management of older organizations, would seem to limit sycophancy by providing fewer opportunities for it. And wouldn't the "disruptive innovation" celebrated by this new system, with its supposed reliance on data and embrace of change, represent the death knell for the sycophancy so common in the old patron-client systems? Why suck up when the system is being torn down?

But even so atomized a workplace has, as the IM literature gracelessly puts it, "leverage points" that allow the ambitious to "successfully execute ingratiation strategy." In fact, the so-called "gig economy" might well intensify sycophancy. Employers who once valued loyalty, experience, and knowledge of a particular company might well find flexibility, the fresh perspective guaranteed by a steep learning curve, and the obedience of a can-do attitude a better fit. The gig economy requires continuous self-presentation, the creation and maintenance of a persona ingratiating enough to be hired again and again.

Even consultants, the shock troops of our current economic transformation who embody the hyper-rationalist spirit of creative destruction, must get hired. Every pitch, every reorganization plan or right-sizing scheme, offers an occasion for impression management, for toadying and false promises. All the consultant need do is tell the client what the client wants to hear—that some form of cost-cutting will increase profits in the short run, or at least raise the stock price.[7] The form of the workplace or the structure of society might vary, but sycophancy seems to find a place within any design for living.

This gloomy conclusion brings us back to literature. As the poet and social commentator Matthew Arnold wrote, literature is fundamentally a "criticism of life." A "criticism"—not a prescription or a cure. The range and scope of literature's meditation on sycophancy reminds us that the question is less "What to do?" than "How does sycophancy shape our dealings with others?"

While the ultimate motivations and intentions of a particular sycophant might never be accessible, literature allows us to imagine the range of sycophantic types, from the small, hard ego of those who follow their interests narrowly as they flatter, to the nullity of the flunky who mimics his target to fill an emptiness within. It shows how vulnerable we are to blandishment, and how ingenious sycophants can be. Through literature, we recognize the specious appeal of the "sycophant within": that sucking up can be regulated—taken up and abandoned without essential change to the character of the sycophant. Literature demonstrates how such a vice can become entangled with more laudable pursuits, such as the development of independence and autonomy, the expansion of the imagination, or the kindling of an artistic sensibility. But above all, literature reminds us of how much we lose in tolerating sycophancy: ingratiation falsifies the terms of our engagement with others, the fundamental basis of the communities we inhabit.

The Apotheosis of Sycophancy

Still, despite the corruption and damage of this vice, we cannot help but savor egregious acts of sycophancy. The descendants of Austen's Reverend Collins are yet with us, and lately, they bow, scrape, and strut on an arguably larger scale. The 2016 election of Donald Trump, a world-class enabler of sycophants and an estimable sycophant himself, has made this clear. Reporters and pundits have mostly noted the sycophants around "The Donald"—the troop of job seekers and flunkys who rallied to him during his campaign. We've followed the humiliations of House Speaker Paul Ryan, as he again and again put his conscience in his pocket to back the president-elect (fortunately his conscience seems small and easily compacted, and he does not seem to miss it overmuch). We watched Mitt Romney, who categorically denounced Candidate Trump as a "phony" and a "fraud," interview for a post in the new administration, posing for awkward pictures as he dined, oligarch style, with the boss at Jean-Georges in Trump Tower. And of course there was Chris Christie, whose descent from presidential contender to toady spokesman for Trump to silent stage prop to convenient butt of his childish fat-jokes seemed destined to be completed by impeachment or even indictment in the wake of the so-called Bridgegate scandal. Even as we write, the stakes seem to be going up for Trump's sycophants, who appear at a loss for adequate words in which to convey their feelings. When Kellyanne Conway received the pseudo-office of "counselor to the president" from her boss, she was quick to abase herself. Thanks would have been adequate, or even the simple registration of gratification, but public fawning seems to be required by the new regime. Ms. Conway reported herself "humbled and honored" in a statement, but then, swept up by the force of her feelings in an interview on the same day, she pronounced herself "just really pleased and frankly very humbled." Surely we are in the presence of an estimable sycophant: Ms. Conway deserves extra marks for that teasing "frankly," a sure sign that the statement to follow is dubious. Finally, the newly appointed "counselor," yet again unable to contain her feelings of humility and unworthiness, went on Twitter to say "Grateful & humble, @realDonaldTrump." Although her words seem formulaic and unimaginative, we should not underestimate this achievement—any more than we should understate the cumulative force of Uriah Heep's cloying "umble." And Ms. Conway goes Heep one better. In one day, Ms. Conway managed to crawl in three distinct media—a print statement, a televised interview, and Twitter. Truly the triple crown of flattery.

Mr. Bennet soon found the pleasures of such humor cloying; we too can look at only so much. But the Trump era promises something additional: not simply round-the-clock political sycophancy but the calculated display of such abasement. Almost as soon as the surprise of the election faded, the nation, and even the world, was treated to a real-time record of sycophancy on parade. A live feed from Trump Tower registered entrances and exits of various job-hunting flatterers making the slow march through the lobby to the elevator. The blank lens, with its amateurish framing and refocusing, the undefined space of the lobby, and the incoherent buzz of the crowd give the walk a dreamy unreality. The prospective suck-ups seem to float toward the desk like downed and stranded dirigibles, nosing this way and that as they await rescue. While we can only imagine the feelings of the supplicants as they experience their ascent to the garishly opulent Trump suite, we can certainly relish the difficulties of the aspirants in striving to maintain a sense of dignity as they negotiate the lobby. The privacy and seclusion of the elevator must feel welcome, as one faux populist after another is reduced, by the indiscriminate gaze of the camera, to a figure in the crowd. (At last, a bit of democracy, although of a negative variety!) Surely most have done their share of kissing the ring in their long careers in business and politics, but here the obeisance is public, and their humiliation takes the form of a triumphal possession. But unlike the captives who had pride of place in Roman triumphs—ahead of the display of loot, exotic treasures, or curiosities—there are no chains here. The coercion is inward, the regulation internal. And the live feed at Trump Tower records a strangely modern variant of sycophancy—the object of abasement remains at a remove, above, waiting, perhaps even watching his sycophants arrive on the Internet. Digital sycophancy has arrived.

Sycophancy has always been with us. The question, as ever, remains. Will we see it as a character flaw, reprehensible action by an individual, or will we recognize it, as Dante did, for what it is: a fraudulence that weakens and destroys the community in which we act? Sowing distrust, encouraging cynicism, confounding truth with lies, sycophancy coexists with all the frauds of Dante's Malebolge: hypocrisy, lying, seduction, pimping, theft, false prophecy, the sowing of discord, and counterfeiting. To confront sycophancy—and its enablers—is to engage in a struggle over the very nature of reality. May we prove equal to the task!

ACKNOWLEDGMENTS

One of the most amusing aspects of writing this book was discussing sycophancy with friends. When Fanny Brice first meets Billy Rose in the film *Funny Lady,* she quips, "And if we all hate the same people, it's a match." Shared dislike is a powerful bonding agent, and we had many such "matches." We would like to thank the friends whose lively conversation helped sharpen our thinking on the subject—Peter Manning, Anne Kinney, Kendon Stubbs, John Miller, Ellen Zhang, the late Donald L. Shaw, Jerome McGann, Eileen Heaslip, Julie Eng, Clare Carroll, and James La-Force. Anne Kinney and Ellen Zhang provided us with some juicy examples of flatterers from Chinese lore. We would also like to thank the editorial staff at the University of Virginia Press, especially Eric Brandt and Boyd Zenner, and our agent, Scott Mendel, for their enthusiasm for this project.

NOTES

"FITTEST IMP OF FRAUD"

1. John Milton, *Complete Poems and Major Prose*, ed. Merritt Hughes (Indianapolis: Bobbs-Merrill, 1957), bk. 9, lines 163–68, hereafter cited parenthetically in the chapter text.

WORD SOUNDS AND HISTORIES

1. Aristophanes, *Plutus*, in *Aristophanes: The Eleven Comedies*, 2 vols. (New York: Horace Liveright, 1928), 2:461, 462.

CAUTIONARY TALES

1. We are indebted to Cong Ellen Zhang for this anecdote and the translation.

2. Dante Alighieri, *Inferno*, trans. Allen Mandelbaum (New York: Bantam, 1984), 18.121–22, hereafter cited parenthetically in the chapter text.

3. Walter Isaacson, *Kissinger: A Biography* (New York: Simon and Schuster, 1992), 70.

4. Ibid., 79.

5. Kissinger qtd. ibid., 134.

6. Ibid., 577.

7. Ibid., 191.

8. Ibid., 146–47. See also *The Nixon Tapes: 1971–1972*, ed. Douglas Brinkley and Luke A. Nichter (New York: Houghton Mifflin Harcourt, 2014), where Kissinger, speaking about Soviet Jews, states: "It's none of our business. If they complain—if they made a public protest to us about the treatment of Negroes, we'd be . . . " Nixon responds, "Yeah" (359). For Nixon's comments about the prevalence of Jews among journalists, see ibid.

9. Conversations from Nixon Tapes cited in George Lardner Jr., "New Tapes Reveal Depth of Nixon's Anti-Semitism, http://www

.washingtonpost.com/wp-srv/politics/daily/oct99/nixon6.htm. See also *The Nixon Tapes: 1971–1972*, ed. Brinkley and Nichter, 359–60.

10. The log on this conversation begins on page 323 in this table from the Nixon Library: https://www.nixonlibrary.gov/forresearchers/find/ tapes/finding_aids/tapesubjectlogs/oval866.pdf. To hear the conversation, go to 866-16 in this list: the comment appears at the 13:56 mark. https://www.nixonlibrary.gov/forresearchers/find/tapes/tape866/ tape866.php.

11. Clyde Haberman, "Decades Later, Kissinger's Words Stir Fresh Outrage among Jews," *New York Times,* December 16, 2010, http://www .nytimes.com/2010/12/17/nyregion/17nyc.html.

12. See http://www.newsmax.com/InsideCover/Kissinger-Nixon-Holocaust-Jews/2010/12/27/id/381127/. For comments from Jewish organizations, see, for example, http://torah.org/interest/nixon-kissinger/ and Christopher Hitchens's articles on the subject: http://www.slate.com/ articles/news_and_politics/fighting_words/2010/12/how_can_anyone_ defend_kissinger_now.html; http://hotair.com/headlines/ archives/2010/12/28/have-you-no-shame-mr-kissinger/.

13. Isaacson, *Kissinger,* 147, 494.

THE SCIENCE OF SYCOPHANCY

1. Edward E. Jones, *Ingratiation: A Social Psychological Analysis* (New York: Appleton-Century-Crofts, 1964), hereafter cited parenthetically in the chapter text.

2. Edward E. Jones, *Interpersonal Perception* (New York: W. H. Freeman, 1990), 177; hereafter cited parenthetically in the chapter text.

3. Long-Zeng Wu, Ho Kwong Kwan, Li-Qun Wei, and Jun Liu, "Ingratiation in the Workplace: The Role of Subordinate and Supervisor Political Skill," *Journal of Management Studies* 50.6 (2013): 992, hereafter cited parenthetically in the chapter text.

4. Elaine Chan and Jaideep Sengupta, "Insincere Flattery Actually Works: A Dual Attitude Perspective," *Journal of Marketing Research* 47 (2010): 122–33, hereafter cited parenthetically in the chapter text.

5. Karin Proost, Bert Schreurs, Karel DeWitte, and Eva Derous, "Ingratiation and Self-Promotion in the Selection Interview: The Effects of Using Single Tactics or a Combination of Tactics on Interviewer Judgments," *Journal of Applied Social Psychology* 40.9 (2010): 2155–69.

6. Nicholas Roulin, Adrain Bangerter, and Julia Levashina, "Interviewers' Perceptions of Impression Management in Employment Interviews," *Journal of Managerial Psychology* 29.2 (2014): 141–63.

7. Mark Bolino, Anthony Klotz, and Denise Daniels, "The Impact of Impression Management over Time," *Journal of Managerial Psychology* 29.3 (2013): 266–84, hereafter cited parenthetically in the chapter text.

8. Yongmei Liu, Gerald R. Ferris, Jun Xu, Barton A. Weitz, and Pamela L. Perrewe, "When Ingratiation Backfires: The Role of Political Skill in the Ingratiation-Internship Performance Relationship," *Academy of Management Learning and Education* 13.4 (2014): 570, hereafter cited parenthetically in the chapter text.

LITERATURE AND SYCOPHANCY

1. *Plutarch's Moralia*, trans. Frank Cole Babbitt (New York: Putnam's Sons, 1927), 265, hereafter cited parenthetically in the chapter text.

2. William Shakespeare, *The Riverside Shakespeare*, ed. G. Blakemore Evans (New York: Houghton Mifflin, 1997), 3.2.376–82, hereafter cited parenthetically in the chapter text.

3. Jane Austen, *Pride and Prejudice*, ed. R. W. Chapman (Oxford: Oxford University Press, 1982), 63, hereafter cited parenthetically in the chapter text.

4. Jane Austen, *Sense and Sensibility*, ed. R. W. Chapman (Oxford: Oxford University Press, 1982), 376, hereafter cited parenthetically in the chapter text.

5. Charles Dickens, *Great Expectations*, ed. Janice Carlisle (New York: Bedford, 1996), 153, hereafter cited parenthetically in the chapter text.

6. Charles Dickens, *David Copperfield* (London: Penguin, 1996), 689, hereafter cited parenthetically in the chapter text.

7. J. R. R. Tolkien, *The Two Towers* (Boston: Houghton Mifflin, 1982), 118.

8. J. R. R. Tolkien, *The Return of the King* (Boston: Houghton Mifflin, 1982), 299.

SYCOPHANCY AS AN ART FORM

1. Baldassare Castiglione, *The Book of the Courtier*, ed. Daniel Javitch (New York: Norton, 2002), 80, hereafter cited parenthetically in the chapter text.

2. Christopher Hibbert, *Disraeli: The Victorian Dandy Who Became Prime Minister* (New York: Palgrave Macmillan, 2006), 271.

3. Wilde qtd. ibid., 285.

4. Robert Blake, *Disraeli* (New York: St. Martin's, 1967), 491.

5. See http://www.pbs.org/empires/victoria/empire/gladstone.html.

6. William Kuhn, *The Politics of Pleasure: A Portrait of Benjamin Disraeli* (London: Free Press, 2006), 291.

7. Robert O'Kell, *Disraeli: The Romance of Politics* (Toronto: University of Toronto Press, 2013), 448.

8. Kuhn, *The Politics of Pleasure*, 483.

9. Blake, *Disraeli*, 546.

10. O'Kell, *Disraeli: The Romance of Politics*, 551n17.

11. "Disraeli's Flowery History," https://history.blog.gov.uk/2013/04/29/disraelis-flowery-history/.

12. Blake, *Disraeli*, 749–50.

13. Kate Williams, *England's Mistress: The Infamous Life of Emma Hamilton* (New York: Random House, 2009), 108, hereafter cited parenthetically in the chapter text. Lady Hamilton, like many of those in the class to which she aspired, was an indifferent speller. We have quoted from her letters as they stand.

TRANSFORMATIVE SYCOPHANCY

1. Marcel Proust, *Swann's Way*, trans. Scott Moncrieff et al. (New York: Modern Library, 1992), 181, hereafter cited parenthetically in the chapter text.

2. Marcel Proust, *Within a Budding Grove*, trans. Scott Moncrieff et al. (New York: Modern Library, 1992), 68, hereafter cited parenthetically in the chapter text.

3. Marcel Proust, *The Guermantes Way*, trans. Scott Moncrieff et al. (New York: Modern Library, 1992), 367, hereafter cited parenthetically in the chapter text.

4. Patricia Highsmith, *The Talented Mr. Ripley, Ripley Under Ground, Ripley's Game* (New York: Knopf, 1999), 8, hereafter cited parenthetically in the chapter text.

HOW LOW CAN ONE GO?

1. Lauren Weisberger, *The Devil Wears Prada* (New York: Doubleday, 2003), 302, hereafter cited parenthetically in the chapter text.

2. Kazuo Ishiguro, *The Remains of the Day* (New York: Vintage International, 1993), 42, hereafter cited parenthetically in the chapter text.

3. Salman Rushdie, *The Satanic Verses* (New York: Picador, 1988), 7, hereafter cited parenthetically in the chapter text.

4. The translation is by Angelika Powell, the former Slavic librarian at the University of Virginia's Alderman Library.

5. Niccolò Machiavelli, *The Prince*, trans. W. K. Marriott (London: Dent, 1928), 186, hereafter cited parenthetically in the chapter text.

6. Earl of Chesterfield, *Chesterfield's Letters to His Son*, http://www .gutenberg.org/ebooks/3361. Letters from this work are subsequently cited in the chapter text by their date.

7. This might seem a harsh assessment, but until one hears of consultants who recommend hiring more workers, expanding (or even maintaining) benefits, and raising wages, it seems fair. Richard Sennett's dismissive characterization of consultancy, "authority without responsibility," is perfectly apt (Sennet, *The Culture of New Capitalism* [New Haven: Yale University Press, 2006], 1).

INDEX

Illustrations are indicated by italicized page numbers.

North, Thomas, 33

obscene gesture associated with
original derivation of term
"sycophant," 8
obsequiousness, 1, 10, 24, 29, 45,
78, 86–87, 98, 104
original sin's relationship to sycophancy, 4–5
origins of sycophancy, 7–8
"owes it to himself" behavior, 5

Parma, Duke of, 9
performative nature of sycophancy, 56–59, 74. *See also* film's
depiction of sycophancy
Plutarch: on discerning cause
of why something is said, 32;
"How to Tell a Flatterer from a
Friend," 31–33, 58, 59, 60, 64,
71, 93, 96, 107; *Lives*, 22, 31, 33;
Moralia, 31; *The Parallel Lives*,
33; Shakespeare's adaptations
of, 33–35
press agent's job, 77, 80
probability of success of sycophant's behavior, 22–27, 44, 77
Proust, Marcel: *The Guermantes
Way*, 88; *In Search of Lost Time*,
84–89; *Swann's Way*, 85; *Within
a Budding Grove*, 88
pulp fiction, 89–95
punishment for flattery, 11, 12–14,
44, 79

quid pro quo model, 2, 24, 64, 84,
92, 102

racial discrimination and stereotypes, 103
Renaissance man, 57

resistance to sycophancy, 104–6,
108
response to sycophancy, 1, 104–12
Reynolds, Joshua, 68
Ritter, Thelma, 75
Romney, George, 66–68; *Sensibil-
ity*, 67
Romney, Mitt, 110
Rowton, Lord, 65
Royal Titles Act (1876), 63
Rushdie, Salman: *The Satanic
Verses*, 101–4
Ryan, Paul, 110

sadism, 77, 79
Saint-Simon's *Memoirs*, 9
Satan as serpent introducing
sycophancy in dealings with
Eve, 4–5
science of sycophancy, 20–30;
beliefs of sycophant and target,
21; challenges of studying, 21,
23–24; disparity in power status
between sycophant and target,
22; identification of types of
ingratiation, 20; Impression
Management (IM), 20, 26–30,
108–9; interpersonal nature of
ingratiation, 21; Jones's study
of ingratiation, 20–25; research
methods, 25, 29–30; shame's
effect, 24–25; sincerity as factor,
25
self-consciousness of sycophancy,
53, 99–100
selfishness as reason to transgress
boundaries, 5
self-loathing, 96
self-love, 31, 32
self-made man, 94–95
self-nullification, 98, 101